AF505078

Staging Marriage in
Early Modern Spain

Staging Marriage in Early Modern Spain

Conjugal Doctrine in Lope, Cervantes, and Calderón

Gabriela Carrión

Lewisburg
BUCKNELL UNIVERSITY PRESS

Published by Bucknell University Press
Co-published with The Rowman & Littlefield Publishing Group, Inc.
4501 Forbes Boulevard, Suite 200, Lanham, Maryland 20706
www.rowmanlittlefield.com

Estover Road, Plymouth PL6 7PY, United Kingdom

British Library Cataloguing in Publication Information Available

Library of Congress Cataloging-in-Publication Data

Carrión, Gabriela, 1963–
   Staging marriage in early modern Spain : conjugal doctrine in Lope, Cervantes, and Calderón / Gabriela Carrión.
      p. cm.
   Includes bibliographical references and index.
   ISBN 978-1-61148-052-8 (cloth : alk. paper) — ISBN 978-1-61148-053-5 (electronic)
   1. Spanish drama—Classical period, 1500–1700—History and criticism. 2. Marriage in literature. 3. Theater—Spain—History—16th century. 4. Theater—Spain—History—17th century. 5. Vega, Lope de, 1562–1635.—Criticism and interpretation. 6. Cervantes Saavedra, Miguel de, 1547–1616.—Criticism and interpretation. 7. Calderón de la Barca, Pedro, 1600–1681.—Criticism and interpretation. I. Title.

   PQ6105.C374 2011
   862'.3093543—dc22
                                            2011003311

∞™ The paper used in this publication meets the minimum requirements of American National Standard for Information Sciences—Permanence of Paper for Printed Library Materials, ANSI/NISO Z39.48-1992.

Printed in the United States of America

In memoriam
Jennifer J. Day

Contents

Acknowledgments

First and foremost, I want to thank Mary Gaylord for tirelessly sharing her wisdom and optimism with me over the years. She saw this project in its first version as a dissertation at Harvard University where she provided me with a source of inspiration to last many lifetimes. Her generosity extends far beyond the dictates of reason and for that I am deeply grateful.

While at Harvard, I also received precious feedback on this project from Abby Zanger who patiently combed through its first drafts. Thanks also to Anthony J. Cascardi at the University of California at Berkeley for being the first to spark my passion for all things Cervantine. Dru Dougherty encouraged me to pursue my studies of literature and offered his kind and patient support at every turn. Thanks also go to Emilie Bergmann for illuminating my first incursions into seventeenth-century Spain.

To my colleagues at Bard College I owe a special debt of gratitude. It is no exaggeration to say that Marina van Zuylen's generosity and humor have kept me afloat throughout this project. Her irrepressible wit has been a constant source of inspiration in both good and bad times. I am deeply grateful to Geoff Sanborn and Sarah Towers for their unfailing support and the warm hospitality they have provided to my entire family. Deirdre d'Albertis and James Romm deserve special thanks for going above and beyond the call of duty; I cannot thank them enough for their extraordinary professionalism. Melanie Nicholson offered her keen insight into the manuscript, and I am grateful for her comments. Odile Chilton made sure that all the French accents were in the right place, and Eric Trudel makes life a joy, regardless of the circumstances. Stephanie Kufner, Florian Becker, Youssef Yacoubi, Tamar Khitarishvili, and Mark Lambert have provided encouragement for which I am truly thankful.

Isabel Arredondo, Emi Morita, Maribel Moheno, Karina Galperín, Belén Pascual Medrano, Cindy Kubick, Amelia Moser, José Luis Blondet, Victor Figueroa, Max Hernández, Luis Casado, Rob Schott, Monique Saigal, Henry Berg, and Lois and Mark Wurmbrand deserve special thanks for many, many years of friendship.

John Sepúlveda and Veronica Lamaison provide a cherished home in whatever country they happen to be living—*gracias de todo corazón.*

I am extremely fortunate to have had the expert readers at Bucknell University Press share their comments on the manuscript. The Program for Cultural Cooperation with the Spanish Ministry of Education, Culture and Sports provided valuable assistance for research in the Biblioteca Nacional in Madrid as did a grant from the Real Colegio Complutense at Harvard University.

My parents have provided me with every sort of encouragement, and I am permanently indebted to them for coming to the rescue at every turn. My sister's piquant humor sustains me, even at a distance. Most of all, my husband Salva has given me every reason to revisit my initial skepticism regarding the institution of marriage. I dedicate this book to him and to our son Diego.

Introduction

Engaging Marriage in Early Modern Spain

In one of the most riveting scenes of Pedro Calderón de la Barca's drama *La vida es sueño*, Rosaura, one of the main protagonists, goes to extraordinary lengths to hold her former suitor to a promise of marriage. Specifically, she casts her fortune with prince Segismundo, precipitating a conflict of staggering political dimensions leading to war. In the final act, she explains to him that she is not only a victim of a false promise of marriage, but also born out of wedlock:

> Deste, pues, mal dado nudo
> que ni ata ni aprisiona,
> o matrimonio o delito,
> si bien todo es una cosa,
> nací yo . . .[1]
>
> [The promise of marriage is like a knot
> that's badly tied, it does not bind,
> it gives no shelter nor protection,
> but I was born from it.][2]

With a breathtaking economy of words, Rosaura summarizes the power marriage wields throughout the Spanish drama. She points to marriage's failure to bind its participants in any effective manner, although it is not the institution itself with which she finds fault. Rather, excessive faith in her suitor's promise of marriage has led her to bed without being wed. Like many heroines before and after her, Rosaura seeks marriage as a means of legitimizing her place in society, despite her eloquent critique of this "badly tied" knot. In the end, she wins the marriage she seeks, but it comes at a considerable price, for the sexual tension that exists between Rosaura and the prince is missing altogether in her final conquest. By all appearances, Segismundo—and not her suitor Astolfo—represents the source of erotic desire, the *real* love interest in the drama. So, while the expedient marriages that take place at the conclusion of *La vida es sueño* serve to reestablish social and political order, they do so at the price of individual desire.

Staging Marriage in Early Modern Spain examines the very promises to which Rosaura gives voice, that is, to the cyclical nature of nuptial vows made and broken appearing throughout the Spanish drama. Miguel de Cervantes, Lope de Vega, and Pedro Calderón de la Barca, among many others, regularly represent marriage in their dramatic works either as the starting point of tragedy or as the "happy end" of comedy, suggesting the centrality of the conjugal bond. As a result, one of the questions this study addresses is why the formulaic nature of these beginnings and endings depends on a promise of marriage. What is it about the union between two individuals that makes for compelling drama? And why is the stage an especially attractive space in which to represent the vicissitudes of marriage in early modern Spain? The range of characters engaging marriage regardless of their gender, class, or race also invites reflection, for matrimony in the Spanish *comedia* represents a source of conflict not only relegated to disputes between husbands and wives, but also to suitors and would-be spouses, parents and their offspring, kings and their subjects.

Those who were banned from marrying in early modern Spain—mainly members of the clergy required to observe a vow of chastity—were exceptional. Such a prohibition was subject to serious dispute that in turn provided additional material for dramatists. For example, in Tirso de Molina's *Marta la piadosa* (1614), the playwright uses the subject of clerical celibacy for satirical ends. When Marta declares she will become a nun, she does so in order to pursue a husband of her own choice rather than the *senex* figure her father has chosen for her. She does not desire to be the symbolic bride of Christ but rather the spouse of a real, flesh and blood man. That the convent or the conjugal life represents the only legitimate institutions available to women during this period does not render her choice irrelevant. On the contrary, marriage appears as the most desirable—if less pious—option. As *Marta la piadosa* suggests, the institution of marriage in early modern Spain is, in large measure, problematic because virtually every Christian, with the exception of the clergy is expected to contract nuptials early in their lifetime.[3]

The Council of Trent (1545–1563) represents one of the most visible attempts to reform Church practices in the sixteenth century, and its twenty-fourth session known as *Tametsi* ("Although") centers on marital legislation.[4] Of the key factors motivating its dictates, clandestine marriages take a prominent place. Before the Council of Trent, to *say* one consented to marriage was indeed enough to *be* married, although such practices were frowned upon. Still, a couple who exchanged vows in private without parental or ecclesiastical consent was, in effect, considered married since the promise of marriage was presumably made before God. The Council, however, declares this practice illegitimate, resulting in what Justina Ruiz de Conde refers to as the birth of clandestine relations: "La clandestinidad no lo es hasta el Concilio de Trento" (Clandestinity does not exist until the Council of Trent.)[5] While the Council's canons consider that anyone entering into marriage without the sanction of the Church lives in a "state of damnation," they also recognize the Church's limitations in identifying and controlling practices it deems anathema. In stating that "the Church does not judge what is hidden," the Council admits a degree of powerlessness to control the secret exchange of nuptial promises.[6] However, rather than disregard practices over which it has no control, the Church actually increases its vigilance.[7] The Council thus demands that all marriages be announced beforehand and then recorded for posterity, rendering public scrutiny a primary condition for contracting marriage.[8] As of the Council of Trent, marriage thus requires a public forum not unlike a theatrical stage with its requisite actors and spectators.

The process of betrothal by which a couple is engaged and wedded in the early modern period thus takes place in a public forum as a way to prevent clandestine relations. The public announcement of a couple's engagement and the subsequent celebration of their nuptials constitute practices that have by now become customary. Less familiar is the lack of privacy surrounding the act of consummating the marriage. Natalie Zemon Davis provides a vivid portrait of just such a moment after a wedding ceremony in the Basque region of sixteenth-century France:

> a wedding procession went back to the house of Sanxi Guerre [the groom's father], where in Basque fashion the young lord of the household would expect to live with the old. After an evening of banqueting, the couple was escorted to Bertrande's marriage bed. Into their room at midnight burst the young village revelers, led by Catherine Boëri, a relative of the curate of Artigat. She was carrying their "*resveil.*" Heavily seasoned with herbs and spices, the drink would ensure the newlyweds ardent mating and a fertile marriage.[9]

These practices reflect the bawdy aspects of conjugal relations that make a regular appearance on the Spanish stage, particularly in the short comic works known as *entremes, mojigangas,* and *jácaras.* Moreover, this lack of privacy is not confined to the comic works of the stage, but represents a commonplace at least as old as Juan Manuel's *El conde Lucanor* (1335).[10] This commonplace also appears in moral treatises that warn against the excesses of raucous wedding celebrations.[11] Taken together, these sources suggest that marital relations were public affairs in which intimacy plays a relatively minor role.

The right to freely contract the conjugal bond is not self-evident during the sixteenth century, despite efforts to protect its consensual status. The Council of Trent's canons explicitly condemn the use of coercion where the choice of spouse is concerned: "the holy council commands all, of whatever rank, dignity and profession they may be, under penalty of anathema to be incurred *ipso facto,* that they do not in any manner whatever, directly or indirectly, compel their subjects or any others whomsoever in any way that will hinder them from contracting marriage freely."[12] Despite these dictates, the right to freely contract marriage remained in question until much later in Spain. The Constitutions of Cádiz of 1812 continued to protect a parent's right to arrange marriages, despite protestations on the part of legislators.[13] Similarly, the right to dissolve marriage was not possible in Spain until the twentieth century, rendering Cervantes's *El juez de los divorcios* (*The Divorce Court Judge*) of 1615 all the more remarkable.[14] If we take into consideration that the right to exercise free will in marriage is not relegated to the imaginary worlds of the drama in early modern Spain, we can begin to understand why the subject engages dramatists and spectators alike. According to Emile Telle, "marriage was the geometric center of society's moral, social, economic, physiological and spiritual concerns."[15] Indeed, conjugal relations—and the obligations incurred with said relations—receive unprecedented scrutiny during the sixteenth century, as evidenced by the proliferation of manuals, sermons, and treatises on the subject.[16]

The didactic literature devoted to marriage provides a particularly apt point of departure for this study, because it prescribes conjugal behavior in far more explicit terms than its literary counterparts. The high rhetorical pitch of sixteenth-century guides to the married life suggests a kind of crisis that extends beyond the institution of marriage itself to encompass the crisis of faith in Counter Reformation Europe.[17] At stake in these disputes over the subject of marriage is the right to exercise free will when choosing a mate in the face of social, economic, and political pressures to do otherwise.[18] Just as importantly, didactic works provide insight into the moral values their authors hold in esteem and shed light on the virtues and vices the moralists associate with virginity, chastity and celibacy. In some cases, these works share the language of the drama; for example, Erasmus's *Colloquys* and Pedro de Luxán's *Coloquios matrimoniales* include female characters who debate the relative virtues of the conjugal bond in lively dialogue form.

In Erasmus's colloquy, "Proci et puellae" (Courtship), to cite one example, a young woman resists marriage by claiming that chastity represents a more virtuous state than marriage; however, her suitor insists they can be chaste even within the confines of the conjugal bond:

> PAMPHILUS. A maiden is something charming, but what's more unnatural than an old maid? Unless your mother had been deflowered, we wouldn't have this blossom here. But if, as I hope, our marriage will not be barren, we'll pay for one virgin with many.

> MARIA. But they say chastity is a thing most pleasing to God.

> PAMPHILUS. And therefore I want to marry a chaste girl, to live chastely with her. It will be more a marriage of minds than of bodies. We'll reproduce for the state; we'll reproduce for Christ. But how little will this marriage fall short of virginity! And perhaps some day we'll live as Joseph and Mary did. But meantime we'll learn virginity; for one does not reach the summit all at once.[19]

This exchange exemplifies the rhetorical possibilities of dialogue in conveying a moral message, in this case the advantages of marriage over chastity, a point for which Erasmus argues throughout his writings. Dialogue offers the reader more than a single narrative point of view and by extension, a more pluralistic vision of morality. The dynamic nature of dialogue also engages the reader through conversation, and when the subject is marriage, this exchange can, as Stanley Cavell suggests, strike the reader as a "parable of philosophy."[20] Indeed, critical discourse characterizes discussions between spouses in both didactic and dramatic works where marriage plays a central role. Dramatic tension is born out of the possibility that a civil exchange between spouses runs the risk of degenerating into hostile and even dangerous confrontation.

In dialogue it is difficult—if not impossible—to locate, in any absolute sense, an authorial point of view that might lead the reader to condemn the writer for his or her views. In the context of the Counter-Reformation, where even the slightest departure from orthodoxy might be treated with suspicion, the choice of narrative mode is therefore critical. Certainly, Erasmus's critics were not convinced that marriage represents a way to "learn virginity," and took issue with the Pamphilus and Maria colloquy.[21] It is not difficult to view Pamphilus's claim that he will marry in order to "reproduce" for the state and

Christ as a cynical attempt to seduce his virginal interlocutor. Just as important, the inclusion of women's voices in these dialogues might strike the reader as astonishing, not only because women were generally excluded from any kind of serious public discourse, but because Erasmus often represents them as holding the rhetorical upper hand. Pamphilus does not succeed in seducing Maria, but he nevertheless makes a forceful argument in favor of the institution of marriage.

At their most basic level, guidebooks provide a sense of direction. They rest on the claim that the reader can achieve results, such as making friends and influencing people, if only the reader follows the rules the guide prescribes. They also assume that readers may play a greater role in self-determination, and such a possibility, however limited, exercises enormous appeal to a female readership in sixteenth-century Spain. Of course, the claims and authority of such guidebooks remain open to question; nowhere is this more evident than in the sixteenth-century manuals of wifely conduct, often written by male members of the clergy with little or no direct experience of conjugal life. For example, Fray Luis de Leon's dedication to his niece María Varela Osorio in *La perfecta casada* does not shy away from confessing the author's lack of experience in his guide to wives: "le enseñaré, no lo que me enseñó a mí la experiencia pasada, porque es ajena de mi profesión, sino lo que he aprendido en las Sagradas Letras" (I will teach you . . . not what past experience taught me for such experience is foreign to my profession, but what I have learned from the Sacred Scriptures.)[22] Despite Fray Luis's self-professed lack of experience, his work dictates a wife's behavior in the strictest of terms.

One of the greatest ironies underlying prescriptive literature on marriage is its constant advocacy of an institution it already considers ideal. If marriage is the exemplary institution its advocates claim, one may ask why they go to such lengths to defend it. One reason for this defense may be that actual behavior in this period does not reflect the ideals or the idealized women (i.e. obedient daughters, subservient wives, and secluded widows) that these writers hold in utmost regard. In some cases, the minute descriptions of "bad" women offer far more vivid portraits than the exemplary models the reader is presumed to emulate. The cast of female characters exercising agency on the Spanish stage—not to speak of the actresses playing these roles and the women spectators watching them—stand as powerful evidence of an alternate reality. Still, despite the limitations these guides impose on their readers by modern-day standards, we cannot fail to recognize the pedagogical opportunities such guidebooks offered, or at least claimed to offer, if we are to appreciate their appeal in sixteenth- and seventeenth-century Spain.

Apart from the proliferation of manuals, sermons, and treatises devoted to the subject of marriage, many of these works also enjoyed numerous editions and translations, thus indicating a demand for such literature.

Chapter 1 focuses on two figures that stand apart for their defense of the moral values that the institution of marriage presumably embodies: Juan Luis Vives (1492–1540) and Fray Luis de León (1527–1591). Their most significant contemporary on the subject, Desiderius Erasmus (1466–1536), argues for the importance of marriage in works that were considered extremely polemical due to their attacks on members of the clergy, whose sexual behavior contradicted the vows of chastity they were presumed to observe.[23] While Vives's and León's texts shy away from these polemics, Erasmus undoubtedly had an impact on their works by taking the institution of marriage seriously in his writings.[24] Vives's work on women's education, *Instrucción de la mujer Christiana* (1523), and Fray Luis de León's guide dedicated more specifically to married women, *La perfecta casada* (1583), share a number of sixteenth-century commonplaces whereby marriage represents part of a natural and divine order conferring a state of grace second only to chastity. However, their status as *conversos*, that is, Jews who had converted to Christianity as a result of the edict of 1492, set them apart from their European contemporaries.[25] Vives lived the majority of his life in exile as a result of his family's persecution by the Inquisition; Fray Luis was incarcerated by the same institution, and shortly after his release wrote *La perfecta casada*. Given these circumstances, their work's emphasis on the role of marriage and family suggests a desire for security in one of the most turbulent chapters of Spanish history marked by its intolerance of religious and cultural differences.

In many ways, sixteenth-century manuals for wifely conduct constitute an important break with the past by directing attention to a subject that was deemed unworthy, namely women and women's education. These manuals represent a significant shift in a pedagogical tradition that by and large neglected women.[26] However, to characterize these manuals as works that forward women's right to self-determination is misleading. By modern standards, the scope of the restrictions these guides impose on women is astonishing, particularly when they turn to the subject of female sexuality. Even when sanctioned by the institution of marriage, female sexuality represents a source of deep concern—if not outright anxiety—for writers such as Vives and León. As a result, marriage receives a great deal of praise, but is also subject to intense scrutiny and regulation in their writings. Moreover, marriage occupies an anomalous position within Spanish society due to its hybrid status as "both a sacrament of the church and a civil matter."[27]

The Council of Trent reflects the multifaceted aspects of marriage in that it reinforces marriage's sacramental status and as a result, legitimizes sexuality, at least within the confines of the conjugal bond. However, despite efforts by the Council of Trent to regulate marriage and hence elevate the social status of wedded couples, by most sixteenth-century standards, the vow of marriage remains a kind of "second best" alternative to that of chastity. One of the most oft-quoted proverbs of the period claims it is better to wed than to "burn" (*es mejor casarse que abrasarse*), and in many ways, this aphorism reflects the complex attitudes toward marriage during the period. If the price of remaining chaste involves "burning" with desire, so the proverb goes, one might as well marry to put out the fire. And yet, this proverb also assumes chastity's superior status to marriage as the more demanding, and therefore virtuous path to follow in a society where sex carries the stigma of sin.

The strict rules of conduct the marriage manuals impose on their readership offer the ideal pretext for creating conflict on the Spanish stage. Chapter 2 considers the representation of marriage in Lope's *Peribáñez y el Comendador de Ocaña* (1614) in light of the rules governing conjugal behavior. In contrast to didactic literature, *Peribáñez* represents marriage as a sentimental union, possibly even a site of erotic desire. The celebration of nuptial love represents a novelty in seventeenth-century Spain, and writers such as Juan Boscán (1490–1542) who express affection for his wife are exceedingly rare. His "Repuesta de Boscán a don Diego de Mendoza" is exceptional in its unabashed praise of a wife.[28] Until this moment, the loving husband had, for the most part, inhabited the world of comedy as an object of derision. Lope de Rueda (1510[?]–1565), for example, represents just such a husband in his one-act play or *paso* titled *Cornudo y contento* (Cuckolded and Content), in which a wife and her lover dupe an all-too-trusting husband. The basis of the deception is significant because it capitalizes on the Tridentine credo that marriage unifies husband and wife in body and soul. Basing their arguments on this credo, the adulterers convince the husband to take a diuretic originally prescribed for her; if husband and wife are, in fact, "one body" so the argument goes then *his* consumption of the medication will alleviate *her* suffering.[29] The diuretic produces its intended effects on the husband, leaving the adulterers to enjoy their affair. As the title *Cornudo y contento* makes clear, the husband happily participates in his own deception.

The main character of Lope de Vega's *Peribáñez* does not resemble the parody of *Cornudo y contento*. On the contrary, Peribáñez goes to great lengths to protect the nuptial bliss that he and his wife celebrate as newlyweds at the beginning of the dramatic action. Without a trace of irony, Peribáñez praises his blushing bride as the person who best fulfills his desires:

Contigo, Casilda, tengo
cuanto puedo dessear
y sólo el pecho prevengo;
en él te he dado lugar,
ya que a merecerte vengo.[30]

Lope's positive portrayal of the husband figure begs the question of whether it does not, in fact, render the lessons of the didactic literature more palatable to his public, for it is one thing to be told to behave in accordance to the dictates of morality espoused in a guidebook such as Vives's *De officio mariti* and quite another to dramatize them for the broader public. While the expression of nuptial love does not generally form part of the didactic literature, the aims of the moralists may have been forwarded by Lope's innovations on the Spanish stage in ways they might not have necessarily approved.

A common complaint among theater's critics in early modern Spain is the subversion of values that wives were expected to uphold, such as fidelity and obedience. The cleric Ignacio de Camargo, for example, expresses outrage at the public's tacit approval of behavior that presumably flies in the face of morality:

La constancia y fidelidad de una muger casada se llama obstinación y dureza, y la facilidad, correspondencia fina y forzosa pensión del agradecimiento. Apláudese la industria en burlar el cuidado del padre y el marido, como primor y habilidad del ingenio, y como triunfo glorioso del amor, liviandad arrestada en abandonar el decoro.[31]

[Constancy and fidelity in a married woman are called stubbornness and harshness; easy virtue is called refined reciprocity and the obligatory price of gratitude. Audiences applaud efforts to deceive a father and husband for the care and skill it takes and refer to it as the glorious triumph of love, that is, promiscuity intent on abandoning decorum.]

Here, the morality espoused by Camargo clashes with that of the dramatic works. If the staging of marital relations on the sixteenth- and seventeenth-century stage strikes the reader as tame by modern standards, the fire and brimstone rhetoric of moralists such as Camargo suggest quite a different picture. Regardless of the morality espoused by the conduct manuals, dramas such as *Peribáñez* therefore indicate a palpable shift in the representation of marriage in early modern Spain.

Chapter 3 turns to Miguel de Cervantes's interlude or *entremés*, *El juez de los divorcios* (1615), a work that stands in stark contrast to the dignified and even sentimental representation of the conjugal couple in *Peribáñez*. In *El juez de los divorcios*, Cervantes parodies a series of couples who go to court in order to obtain a divorce. Despite their irreconcilable differences, the judge does not grant any of them the divorce they desperately seek, thus rendering the title of the play oxymoronic. While critics disagree on the degree to which *El juez de los divorcios* subverts the prevailing social order, the very *disorder* the characters introduce in the courtroom calls into question the domestic harmony that the didactic literature celebrates. The main source of critical disagreement centers on the *entremés*'s comic framework that practically demands the temporary inversion of the preexisting social order. Indeed, *El juez de los divorcios* provides a forum for husbands and wives to voice their dissatisfaction with their marriage in no uncertain terms. Marriage may, in fact, intensify preexisting social conflicts in which women and heretics play a key role, two of which are crucial to early modern Spain: honor and blood purity. Cervantes casts an ironic eye on the inherent contradictions of these concepts when, for example, a drunkard claims that his status as an "old" Christian guarantees his credibility as a plaintiff in his desperate plea for a divorce.

Perhaps no other playwright portrays the darker side of conjugal relations more poignantly than Calderón in his trilogy of wife-murder plays, *El médico de su honra*, *A secreto agravio, secreta venganza* and *El pintor de su deshonra*. Chapter 4 focuses on *El médico de su honra* (1637), a drama that ends in the violent murder of the wife by the hands of her husband as a result of his real or perceived discovery of her betrayal. While the themes of honor, chastity, and fidelity play a critical role in the dramatic action just as they do in *Peribáñez*, their exposition by Calderón results in far more violence where the conjugal couple is concerned. These works do not represent husbands as objects of derision or of admiration; they are simply and tragically "melancholy wife-murderers."[32] These dramas also cast serious doubt on the precepts intended to protect the sanctity of marriage in the didactic literature of the period. By putting into question the high stakes involved in preserving honor at all cost, namely the murder of a wife by a husband who believes—rightly or wrongly—to have been betrayed by her, these works can hardly claim to sentimentalize conjugal relations, much less hold honor as an incontrovertible moral value.

The final chapter of *Staging Marriage in Early Modern Spain* considers the role of widowhood—the ostensible end of marriage—in Lope's *La viuda valenciana* (1620). While the prescriptive literature governs widows' behavior in the strictest terms, Lope provides his protagonist considerable more latitude. In his version of the figure of the widow, she does not observe the requisite period of mourning but instead flies in the face of convention by actively courting a gallant soon after her husband's death. She dons a mask—one of the most theatrical props—in order to maintain her reputation whenever she encounters her new lover. This mask also makes for scenes of considerable erotic titillation that stand in contrast to the extreme isolation proscribed for widows by manuals such as Vives's *Educación de la mujer cristiana*. Moreover, Lope dedicates *La viuda valenciana* to Marta de Nevares, with whom he maintained adulterous relations and who was herself recently widowed, suggesting the autobiographical nature of this work. This dedication provides a glimpse into the complex relations between Lope's dramatic works and their place in his personal life, for while it recognizes the strictures governing a widow's behavior, it also makes abundantly clear the author's disregard for such rules. Contrary to the belief espoused by the moralists that the bonds of marriage extend beyond the grave, in *La viuda valenciana* a husband's death releases his wife from her conjugal duties resulting in her active pursuit of erotic desires.[33]

The subject of marriage and its attendant practices of courtship, betrothal, and widowhood appear so often on the stage in early modern Spain, that the selection of even a few, representative works presents an especially difficult task. If we consider, for example, the staggering production of a playwright such as Lope, the subject of marriage in his works arguably deserves a book in itself. Just as importantly, the multifaceted nature of his works defies classification under a single, unifying rubric. Similar claims can be made of playwrights such as Calderón and Cervantes whose dramatic works offer compelling and sometimes contradictory representations of the conjugal bond. Therefore, this study is neither limited to a single author nor to a single dramatic genre. Rather, it proposes close readings of very distinct dramatic works, including serious and comic full-length dramas as well as an interlude in order to demonstrate the remarkable ways in which they are in dialogue with didactic works on marriage.

In these dramatists' works, marriage becomes an engaging subject for the spectator as the bitter fruits of matrimonial discord as well as the sweeter delights of nuptial bliss take center stage. Unlike the conduct manuals that attempt to communicate their morality in the most explicit terms possible, the inherent ambiguity of literary language in the dramatic works allow for alternative views of marriage. This is not to say that the Spanish *comedia* represents a radical break with the past or with contemporary views of marriage. While many dramatic works of the period are extraordinary in their modernity by, above all, providing a forum for women's voices, others uphold the prevailing moral code whereby fathers, brothers, and husbands represent the final arbiters in marital decisions. Still, the constant presence of marriage in the *comedia* either as the starting point of tragedy or as the happy end of comedy suggests that there is something more at stake than the formulaic demands of a particular genre. Playwrights' own engagement with artistic freedom is very much at the heart of the staging of marriage on the Spanish stage. So, while these playwrights may not entirely reject Medieval views of spousal relations, there exists a discernable shift in their works whereby sentimental attachments take on greater importance. Spanish playwrights take full advantage of the unique space that the stage represents in order to reenact the conflicts arising from the exercise of free will in marriage.

Erasmus defines marriage as the "principal wellspring that produces the greatest joy or unhappiness among humans," and it is through the representation of these contradictory passions that the Spanish drama acknowledges the deeply personal nature of this bond.[34] If Rosaura's marriage at the conclusion of *La vida es sueño* strikes us as problematic, it may not only have to do with the exigencies that demand the reestablishment of the political and social order, but also with the fact that she exercises extraordinary agency until this moment. *La vida es sueño* suggests that this agency plays as decisive a role in shaping her identity as does the social institution of marriage—even though personal and political prerogatives may be at odds with each other. While she does not express sexual attraction for the man with whom she finally contracts marriage, she wages war to restore her place in society, and she does so on her own terms. Her actions represent an astonishing reversal of the moralists' dictates that women should be neither seen nor heard. Throughout the Spanish drama of the early modern period, the process of fashioning human identity is "resolutely dialectic," that is, individuals define themselves according to—or despite—social institutions.[35] So too, the dramatic works that are the subject of this study suggest a growing recognition of the constant negotiation that takes place between social institutions and individuals when it comes to marriage.

Notes

1. Calderón de la Barca, *La vida es sueño*, lines 2766–70.
2. Calderón de la Barca, *Life Is a Dream*, 86.
3. Jonathan W. Thacker's discussion of *Marta la piadosa* addresses the question of the play's classification as comedy in ways that are directly related to the subject of marriage: "Critics who hesitate before categorizing *Marta la piadosa* fail to stress that Marta's brother's death is in the past, the play's pre-history (her marriage is raised from those ashes), and that her hypocrisy (unlike Tartuffe's to whose it has been compared) is a temporary gambit to forestall her father's plans. Out of death and potential disaster come light and joy, marriage and fecundity." Thacker, "Comedy's Social Compromise," 270.

4. Meehan, Andrew, "The Catholic Encyclopedia." Jesús María Usunáriz summarizes the importance of the Tridentine decrees on marriage: "The matrimonial freedom defended by Trent involved three aspects: the benefit of free consent in marriage, free choice in contracting the conjugal life, and freedom in marriage." Usunáriz, "El matrimonio como ejercicio de libertad en la España del siglo de oro," 168. All translations mine unless otherwise noted.

5. Ruiz de Conde, *El amor y el matrimonio secreto en los libros de caballerías*, 4. This study provides a detailed account of the legal and canonical distinctions regarding different types of conjugal promises before the advent of Trent. According to Ruiz de Conde, many of what appear to be premarital unions in the novels of chivalry were, in fact, considered legitimate marriages. Referring to the sentimental liaisons in Joanot Martorell's *Tirant lo blanc*, Ruiz de Conde explains that "Estefanía-Diafebo, Tirant-Carmesina, are not simply lovers, but in reality couples married according to the laws and customs that previous to the Council of Trent (1545–1563) were accorded to marriages referred to as 'clandestine.'" Ibid., 3.

6. Schroeder, *Canons and Decrees of the Council of Trent*, 183.

7. For example, Bartolomé Bennassar observes a sharp increase in the number of bigamy cases prosecuted by the Inquisition during the years in which the Council of Trent took place: "At last in 1565, the *Suprême* sends a letter to all the courts to remind them of the necessity of punishing polygamists to the full extent of the kingdom's laws. The stricter application of the law of the middle of the sixteenth century is therefore confirmed. If more people are condemned, it is not because there are a greater number of guilty parties. Rather, it is part of the process of emptying a virile abscess. Moreover, the sentences acquire a new public dimension, which systematically consists of an auto-da-fe. There is a tangible desire to make an example, a desire to publicize." Bennassar, *L'Inquisition espagnole, XVe–XIXe Siècle*, 314.

8. Schroeder, *Canons and Decrees of the Council of Trent*, 183.

9. Davis, *The Return of Martin Guerre*, 18. Stephanie Coontz also concludes that the lines dividing public and private spaces are drawn far more broadly during the early modern period: "The rich, along with the lower-class youths who worked as their servants, lived in large households that gave a married couple very little privacy. Even among the middle classes, households typically included servants or lodgers. Few couples could carve out private spaces where they might take their meals, or even conduct their sex lives, discrete from other household members." Coontz, *Marriage, a History*, 128.

10. Juan Manuel's *El conde Lucanor* portrays the public spectacle that constitutes the consummation of wedding vows in the story titled "De lo que contesçió a un maçebo que casó con una [muger] muy fuerte et muy brava." The family members anxiously wait at the couple's door until the groom emerges triumphant as he overcomes his bride's resistance to his domination. Fernando de Rojas' *Celestina* (1499) also offers a number of noteworthy examples of the relative privacy offered to couples.

11. For example, Juan Luis Vives reminds the reader that on the day of the wedding, "ninguna necesidad hay de bailes ni de danzas, ni de aquel estrépito de

banquetes y de descomedidos regocijos, no sea que acontezca lo que dice el Sabio: *La risa se mezclará con el dolor y el llanto moja el calcañar del gozo.* Con mejor acuerdo debiera inaugurarse el nuevo estado con súplicas y con oraciones para que le dé faustos sucesos Aquel en cuya mano está el poder darlos" (there is no need of dancing, round dances, and all that hubbub of drinking and uncontrolled and prolonged gaiety, lest the wise man's words be verified: 'Laughter will be mixed with sadness and grief occupies the last moments of mirth.' Rather, the man and woman should begin with prayers and supplications that he in whose hands they are may grant them a happy outcome). Vives, *The Education of a Christian Woman,* 179.

12. Schroeder, *Canons and Decrees of the Council of Trent,* 189.

13. Tierno Galván, ed., *Actas De Las Cortes De Cádiz,* 293.

14. Divorce in Spain was not legal until 1981, with the exception of a brief period during the Second Republic (1932–1939). Tobio, "Marriage, Cohabitation and the Residential Independence of Young People in Spain," 68.

15. Telle, *Érasme de Rotterdam et le septième sacrement: étude d'evangélisme matrimonial au XVI siècle et contribution a la biographie intellectuelle d'Érasme,* 296.

16. Other Spanish works apart from those by Juan Luis Vives and Fray Luis de León include, Pedro de Luján's *Coloquios matrimoniales,* Juan de Molina's sermón "en loor del matrimonio," and Pedro Mexía who dedicates five chapters to the subject of marriage in *Silva de varia lección.* Outside of Spain, writers on the subject of conjugal relations include Erasmus (*Declamatio in genere suasorio de laude matrimonii, Encomium matrimonii*), Andre Tiraqueau (*De legibus connubialisibus*), Giovanni Nevizanno (*Sylva nuptialis*), and Agrippa Von Nettesheim (*Declamation on the Nobility and Preeminence of the Female Sex, Declamation on the Sacrament of Marriage,* and *The Ladies' Oracle*).

17. Elliott, *Imperial Spain 1469–1716,* 224–31.

18. Usunáriz, "El matrimonio como ejercicio de libertad en la España del siglo de oro," 182.

19. Erasmus Roterodamus, *Collected Works of Erasmus.1469–1536,* 265.

20. Cavell, *Pursuits of Happiness the Hollywood Comedy of Remarriage,* 86. Cavell examines the representation of marriage in film as a point of departure for philosophical inquiry. According to Cavell, the exchange that takes place between the couple in the film *It Happened One Night* parallels and even exemplifies the desire to cultivate the life of the mind: "there may be a bickering that is itself a mark, not of bliss exactly, but say of caring. As if the willingness for marriage entails a certain willingness for bickering." Ibid.

21. "When condemning the *Colloquies* in its *Determinatio* of May 1526 . . . the faculty of theology of Paris made specific objection to several passages in this dialogue. . . . First, it said, by arguing that marriage is superior to virginity, Erasmus outdid Jovinian, whom Jerome opposed. . . . To these criticisms *Erasmus replies by asking first with which of the speakers, Pamphilus or Maria, his critics identify him.* For it is natural that Pamphilus would depreciate virginity in favour of marriage and that Maria, who intends to be married, would nevertheless counter his impatience.

She is unimpressed by his rhetoric about learning virginity through marriage . . . his detractors take Pamphilus too seriously here, and anyway Pamphilus' remarks are not without merit. Certain of his Spanish critics too found fault with 265:17–24 [the exchange quoted above]. Erasmus tells them allowance must be made for Pamphilus' age and ardor and maintains that what is said is both proper and appropriate. Nor are Pamphilus' remarks about chastity and about Joseph and Mary unreasonable. If the conversation of all young lovers were like this one, would the Catholic faith be imperiled? No." Erasmus, *The Colloquies of Erasmus*, note 67. Emphasis added.

22. León, *A Bilingual Edition of Fray Luis De León's La Perfecta Casada*, 6–7.

23. *Institutio Christiani Matrimonii* (1526) constitutes Erasmus's most extensive work on marriage. Other works on the subject include his *Encomium matrimonii* (1518) and the *Colloquia* (1523) on marriage including "Courtship," "The Girl with No Interest in Marriage," "The Repentant Girl," "Marriage," and "The Young Man and the Harlot." Michael J. Heath provides an introduction to these works in his translation of *Institutio Christiani Matrimonii*.

24. Bataillon, *Erasmo y España*, 634–35.

25. For a discussion of the complex set of laws governing the *conversos* see Albert A. Sicroff's *Los estatutos de limpieza de sangre. Controversias entre los siglos XV y XVII*. Of particular relevance is the degree to which marriage further complicated the *conversos'* already difficult circumstances: "Specific measures were taken against the *moriscos* that lived apart from the Christians and retained their identity as a group. Thus, the expulsion of 1609 seemed an adequate means to resolving the problem they represented in Spain. This measure could never have been taken against the Christianized Jews. Marriages had mixed their lineage with that of the Old Christians to such a degree that the Christianized Jews could never have been isolated for expulsion." Sicroff, *Los estatutos de limpieza de sangre*, 44.

26. Howe, *Education and Women in the Early Modern Hispanic World*, 99–105.

27. Heath, "Introductory Note," 205.

28. Juan Boscán writes:
    heme casado con una mujer,
    que es principio y fin del alma mía.
    Ésta me ha dado luego un nuevo ser,
    con tal felicidad que me sostiene
    llena la voluntad y el entender . . .
    El campo que era de batalla, el lecho,
    ya es lecho para mí de paz durable
    dos almas hay conformes en un pecho. . . .
    De manera, señor, que aquel reposo
    que nunca alcancé yo, por mi ventura,
    con mi filosofar triste y pensoso,
    una sola mujer me le asegura,
    y en perfeta sazón me da en las manos
    vitoria general de mi tristura.

[. . . I have married a woman
who is the beginning and end of my soul.
She has now renewed my being
with such happiness that it sustains me
by fulfilling my desire and my understanding . . .
The battleground that was once my bed
is now a bed of enduring peace for me,
two souls united in one breast . . .
Thus sir, the repose that I never,
unfortunately, achieved with my
sad and painful philosophizing,
is now assured by a single woman,
who with perfect timing, places in my hands
complete victory over sorrow.]

In Rivers, *Poesía lírica del Siglo De Oro*, lines 128–69.

29. Rueda, *Pasos*, 133–34.

30. Vega, *Peribáñez y el Comendador de Ocaña*, 71–75.

31. Cotarelo y Mori, *Bibliografía de las controversias sobre la licitud del teatro en España*, 126.

32. Soufas, "Calderón's Melancholy Wife-Murderers," 1.

33. Other works where widows play a central role include Pedro Calderón de la Barca's *La dama duende* and his short, one-act play or *mojiganga* titled *El pésame de la viuda*.

34. Erasmus, *Collected Works of Erasmus*, 215.

35. Greenblatt, *Renaissance Self-Fashioning*, 1.

CHAPTER ONE

~

How to Be Married

The Moralists' Perspective

An Elaborate Proposal: Juan Luis Vives

Juan Luis Vives's work serves an ideal point of departure to examine didactic discourses devoted to marriage, because his manual, *The Education of a Christian Woman* (*Institutio Foeminae Christianae*) provides a systematic educational program for women in which marriage plays a key role. Although *The Education of a Christian Woman* was published a century before the rise of the Spanish *comedia*, numerous editions and translations of this work suggest its continued success well after its first edition of 1523.[1] Given that so few didactic works were dedicated to a readership composed primarily of women during this period, there is reason to believe that *The Education* exercised considerable influence in shaping subsequent attitudes toward women's education in general and marriage in particular.[2] Moreover, as one of the Renaissance's most illustrious humanists, Juan Luis Vives was sought after by some of the most powerful courts of sixteenth-century Europe, including that of Henry VIII and Catherine of Aragon; in fact, Vives dedicates *The Education* to Catherine so that her daughter Mary "will read these recommendations and will reproduce them as she models herself."[3] *The Education* thus offers a unique window to Vives's complex views regarding marriage, although it remains unclear whether his female readership necessarily adhered to the lessons it prescribes given that many of the dramatic works of the following century actually put into question the behavior that *The Education* preaches.

Vives's most significant predecessor on the subject of marriage in early modern Europe was Erasmus, who five years earlier had written a defense

1

of marriage titled *Declamatio in genere suasorio de laude matrimonii* (1518).[4] However, Erasmus's treatment of the subject is directed to an entirely different readership, that is, the clergy who refuses to observe the vow of celibacy. Erasmus's works on marriage may therefore be read as a thinly veiled attack on clerical promiscuity, although his critics were not convinced that works such as the *Encomium matrimonii* were strictly the rhetorical exercises he purported them to be. In fact, the vice-chancellor of the University of Leuven, Jean Briard, declares Erasmus's opinions regarding marriage and celibacy heretical.[5] In contrast to the heated debates regarding the clergy's sexual behavior, Vives's work attempts to establish a strict distance from these polemical issues.

The central book of *The Education of a Christian Woman* is devoted to married women, and here Vives claims to approach the subject objectively by neither praising nor criticizing the institution of marriage:

> No hay lugar aquí de tratar de los loores o vituperios del matrimonio ni hay que tocar acerca de él las añejas cuestiones; verbigracia: si el sabio debe tomar mujer, ni aquellas otras que nuestros autores cristianos suscitaron sobre el matrimonio, el celibato, [y] la virginidad.[6]

> [This is not the place to discuss the praise or blame of marriage or to touch on inveterate questions, such as whether a wise man should take a wife; or those topics treated by our own Christian authors concerning marriage, celibacy, and virginity.][7]

Here, *The Education* raises the controversial issue of celibacy only to dismiss it, but this claim of objectivity will be reversed almost immediately in the same paragraph and again at the conclusion of the chapter where Vives critiques those who reject and anathematize marriage. Moreover, Vives does not elaborate upon the "erroneous" beliefs of the presumed heretics who reject marriage, nor does he rail against those who, in Erasmus's provocative words, "conceal their vices behind the high-sounding name of castration."[8] By attending to those readers who are *already* assumed to participate in the institution of marriage, rather than to those who flout the rules of socially acceptable behavior, Vives distances his text from potential criticism, effectively preaching to the converted.

The Education exalts marriage as "aquella comunicación y amistad universal que nos contiene a todos como hermanos y . . . nos liga con un mutuo afecto" (that universal communication and friendship that binds us all like brothers and . . . joins us in mutual affection).[9] These words hardly suggest a neutral or objective stance; rather, they favor marriage as a simultaneously "natural" and sacred bond that is capable of uniting its participants by responding to the human need for companionship. While Vives follows Erasmus's definition of marriage, the latter's praise for the institution emphasizes another reason it considers fundamental to the construction of the conjugal bond: marriage as the exclusive means to legitimating sexual reproduction: "nothing has been so firmly implanted by nature, not only in mankind but in all living things, as the instinct . . . to preserve its own species from destruction and render it in some way immortal by the propagation of offspring. Everyone must know that this cannot come about without the bond of wedlock."[10] By associating sexual reproduction with marriage, Erasmus naturalizes a social institution. Erasmus goes on to argue that not only do human beings share this desire for "matrimonial union," but plants and precious gems possess this impulse as well. There even exists a "cosmic" union connecting the "heavens turning with continual motion. . . . Does it [heaven] not play the part of a husband as it fructifies the earth, parent of all things, beneath it, making it produce every manner of thing by the infusion of its seed?"[11] The desire for "matrimonial union" is thus placed before human existence in the natural world and not as a consequence of its existence.

It is ironic that so much of a manual such as Vives's *The Education* should be devoted to detailing the precise conditions for contracting marriage given its presumably natural basis. For example, a chapter such as "De cómo se ha de buscar esposo" (How to Seek a Husband) provides specific directions and prohibitions when choosing a spouse, and indicates little of a "natural" order. According to Vives, an eligible young woman should say little, if anything, regarding her future spouse, leaving all decisions regarding marriage in her parents' hands. If, as *The Education* suggests, marriage is part of the natural order as ordained by God, there would be little need to regulate it with such a high degree of specificity. In its attempts to both sanctify and naturalize marriage, *The Education* does just the reverse: it reveals the highly constructed, *social* basis of the institution.

Unlike Erasmus, Vives does not insist on the relationship between marriage and procreation. According to *The Education*, a couple bound by matrimony only needs to procreate, "si les viniere voluntad de ello, puesto que el matrimonio no tanto fue ordenado con vistas a la prole como para una cierta comunidad de vida y sociedad indisoluble" (if a willingness to do so should arise, since marriage was not instituted for the purpose progeny, but rather for a certain communal life and indissoluble society).[12] This emphasis on companionship over procreation is in many regards unorthodox as the latter is conventionally stipulated as one of the principal reasons for entering into marriage. In fact, Vives's aversion to sexuality appears throughout *The Education*, constituting one of its most problematic aspects, particularly as concerns marriage. Does a "certain communal life" constitute sufficient reason for entering into marriage? How are the bonds of friendship or mutual affection ("mutuo afecto") strengthened by a marriage that necessarily excludes desire? Vives, as we will later see, avoids these questions; by his definition, the sanctity of the conjugal bond is of and by itself sufficient reason to love, honor, and obey its terms and conditions.

A number of other features distinguish Vives's treatment of the subject of marriage. All three books of *The Education*, published three years earlier than Erasmus's monumental work, *Institutio Christiani Matrimonii* (1526), devote serious attention to the various stages of marriage, including courtship, betrothal, and widowhood. The fact that Vives would also devote a treatise to the subject of husbands' role in marriage, *De officio mariti* (1528), further attests to his dedication to the subject. Both guides to husbands and wives openly proclaim their didactic content in contrast to many of Erasmus's works where a more ambiguous approach prevails. For example, unlike Erasmus's *Encomium*, which presents an epistle to a young bachelor who resists marriage, *The Education* assumes a girl's full compliance with the lessons it espouses, including a willingness to marry. In this regard, *The Education* has more in common with Erasmus's treatise on boys' education, *De civilitate morum puerilium libellus* (1530), in that both are didactic treatises aimed at shaping social behavior. However, Erasmus makes no mention of marriage in *De civilitate*, published seven years *after* Vives's treatises. More importantly, given Vives's cultural background as a Spaniard and, more specifically, as a *converso*, it is not inconceivable that *The Education* bears a close relation to the moral values of sixteenth-century Spain.[13] The fact that *The Education* was dedicated to the Spanish queen of England, Catherine of Aragon, and that Vives himself was closely associated with her court, were prestigious recommendations to Vives's Spanish-speaking audience.

In *The Education*'s dedication to Catherine, Vives extols her virtues and marvels at her command of Latin.[14] These may have not been idle exercises of *captatio benevolentiae* common to Renaissance writings. Catherine's knowledge of Latin admitted her into the circle of Oxford scholars that included Thomas More, one of her most steadfast defenders in the complex divorce proceedings initiated by her husband, Henry VIII. She never recognized Henry's petition for a divorce and as such put the institution of marriage to a test of international proportions.[15] By honoring the conjugal contract, Catherine laid claim for herself and her daughter to the throne of England. It is not impossible to imagine that *The Education* and its numerous examples of highly literate women drawn from classical, biblical, and contemporary sources bolstered such resistance. The high value Vives ascribes to marriage was consonant with Catherine's claims that denied Henry VIII a divorce. Above all, Catherine's claims conform to the prevailing attitude of the time that the conjugal bond could not be lightly forfeited given its indissolubility.

The most recent and comprehensive critical efforts to articulate Vives's views on women's education place the educational policies advocated by *The Education* within the turbulent circumstances of Vives's life.[16] The fact that Vives's parents were *conversos* suggests why he placed such importance on the institution of marriage, given that the *converso* community considered marriage a fundamental means to preserve faith and culture. According to Juan A. Jorge de García Reyes, Jewish matrimonial laws in Spain were marked by their "strict obligation to everything relative to marriage and family."[17] As a consequence of the political and social turbulence following the edict of 1492 ordering the expulsion or conversion of all Jews from Spain, Vives lived most of his life in exile. While he was able to live safely in exile, the Inquisition persecuted his family; his aunt and her son were burned at the stake for conserving an important synagogue in Valencia, while his father suffered a similar fate between 1524 and 1526.[18]

Until the publication of the documents detailing the trial of Vives's family by Miguel de la Pinta Llorente and José María de Palacio y Palacio in 1962, his exile was understood in strictly academic terms, that is, the University of Paris presumably had a great deal more to offer a budding young intellectual such as Vives than his native Spain. However, the Inquisition's proceedings against Vives's parents—proceedings that continued long after their death— are more convincing explanations of the scholar's exile. After leaving Spain in 1508, Vives never saw either of his parents again: his mother died one year after his departure, and in 1526 his father died in the hands of the Inquisition. It was during this time that Vives wrote *The Education*.

It is difficult to imagine that these events did not have a profound effect on Vives and his writings, particularly those on family, marriage, and women's education. It is likely that he was well acquainted with the vital links between family and culture, given that he himself was compelled by political circumstances to relinquish both. This is not to say that Vives professed such a link with his parents' Judaism; on the contrary, he repeatedly affirms his Christianity. However, the new Christian doctrines espoused by Erasmus on the one hand, and Vives's *converso* background on the other, were not necessarily incompatible ideologies. Moreover, works such as *The Education* appear much more complex and even less retrograde when Vives's own personal history is taken into consideration. Seen in this light, his views, which appear narrow by modern standards, may be understood as an attempt to preserve the distinguishing features of his own culture, his "otherness" in the face of overwhelming adversity and pressure to conform to a culture imposed by a hegemonic power.[19]

In his dedication to Catherine of Aragon, Vives refers to a wide range of authorities, ranging from Aristotle to Augustine, who also wrote on the subject of women's education. According to Vives, these authorities,

> fueron harto escasos en el dar preceptos y normas de vida, pensando ser tarea preferente exhortar a lo mejor y alargar la mano a lo más alto, que humillarse a puntualizar lo más rastrero. Empero nosotros, dando de lado a esas exhortaciones, a fin de que cada cual haga la conveniente elección de su estado, más por la autoridad de ellos que por opinión nuestra, nos proponemos formarlas prácticamente para la vida.[20]

> [gave very few precepts or rules of life, thinking it preferable to exhort their readers to the best conduct and to point the way to the highest examples rather than give instruction about more lowly matters. But leaving exhortation to them so that each may choose for herself a way of life based on their authority rather than on my opinion, I formulate practical rules for living.][21]

While Vives authorizes his work by citing numerous classical and biblical sources, he also outlines those points intended to distinguish his text from the canonical literature that precedes him. According to Vives, these authorities demonstrate little interest in the ordinary circumstances of a women's life and are therefore deficient in defining the precise terms of her education.[22] Vives, in contrast, does not shy away from addressing the more banal aspects of a women's life. His work thus proposes a practical guide to educating women and offers advice on day-to-day subjects ranging from breast-feeding to raising children.[23] *The Education* is, to borrow Stephen Greenblatt's term, a guide to "self-fashioning," designed to help women achieve an exemplary existence. In terms of this model, however, Vives often coincides with his predecessors, referring to their authority throughout *The Education*: "Aquello que no se compadecía con las costumbres generalizadas yo lo sustenté y lo corroboré con grandes autoridades, porque no pudiera derribarlo el empuje del sentimiento general" (Things that would not accord with accepted moral standards I have supported and sustained with the testimony of great authorities, lest they be nullified by the force of public opinion).[24]

The exemplary existence Vives proposes is based on the fundamental stages of a woman's life, which he reduces to childhood, marriage, and widowhood. This reduction reveals the central importance he assigns marriage; by his prescription, childhood is a prologue to marriage and widowhood its epilogue. According to Vives, a woman's childhood and adolescence are intended to prepare her for marriage by developing skills such as sewing and cooking, which will contribute to a harmonious conjugal life. In reference to cooking, to cite one example, Vives writes: "Yo querré que mi mujer sea ducha en este arte, con el cual obligue a cualquiera edad las voluntades de todos lo suyos" (I would prescribe that a woman be practiced in this art so that she may more oblige her dear ones).[25] The first person singular used here is characteristic of *The Education* and indicates Vives's personal ideal of womanhood, notwithstanding his numerous references to classical and biblical sources. The "yo" reflects a far greater subjectivity than his introductory claims to objectivity might lead the reader to expect.

All the characteristics exemplifying the ideal woman are subordinated to the overarching concept of chastity fueling the book's pedagogy. Vives warns his reader that her chastity and reputation are the most valuable possessions of her dowry and adds that even the most insignificant gesture—a sideways glance, a word misspoken, a dance step—may threaten to undermine an otherwise spotless reputation. What might at first sight appear to be the most superficial of these aspects, that is, a woman's apparel, in fact receives inordinate attention in each of the three books of *The Education*. Distinct periods of a woman's life may require different attire, such as mourning dress for a widow. Not surprisingly, *The Education* considers cross-dressing an abomination:

> es razón que así sea, de la vista de aquellos con quienes topamos, pero que también los vestidos lleven consigo las características de aquella diferencia, menester es que nosotros no confundamos aquella en que la Naturaleza puso distinción. Y por todo esto, quien torna el vestido promiscuo, con toda razón es llamado por el Señor abominable, pues que intenta una cosa contraria a la ley natural, que introduciría en la convivencia social un sinnúmero de peligros.[26]

> [we must see to it that our clothes give visible sign of that distinction and do not obscure what nature has clearly marked. Therefore, one who is ambiguous in dress is justly called abominable by the Lord, since he is attempting something that is contrary to the laws of nature, which would give rise to many perils in human society.][27]

Such "visible signs" will play a significant role on the Spanish stage that regularly subverts such strictures for dramatic effect. Lope de Vega, in fact, pardons the break with convention whereby women must not wear men's clothes.[28] Actresses engaged in the practices Vives condemns, such as don men's clothing, dance, and wear makeup, do so as a way to attract the public's attention.

While Vives rejects what he considers superfluous feminine adornments on the grounds that these only serve to deceive the observer, the very basis of the Spanish stage is predicated on such deception.[29]

According to *The Education*, men are guilty of paying excessive attention to a woman's appearance and are thus equally responsible for participating in a game of deception and subsequent seduction. Vives warns his female audience against such a husband, but more significant than the actual warning, is the analogy Vives draws between wives, slaves, and beasts of burden:

> ¿Qué puedes esperar de un marido de esta calaña, a quien contenta más la costra blanca que la esposa buena? ¿Quién llegó jamás a tal grado de mentecatez que, teniendo que comprar un esclavo o un caballo, prefiere que se le muestre engualdrapado que desnudo y con la apariencia misma que le dio la Naturaleza? Y eso que hacemos en los siervos y en las acémilas, ¿no lo hacemos en las esposas?[30]

> [What can you hope for from a man who finds more pleasure in a white encrustation than in a good woman? Who has reached that point of madness that when he is going to buy a slave or a horse he prefers that they be shown to him touched up for sale rather than in their natural state? We do this in the purchase of slaves and beasts of burden; will we not do the same with wives?][31]

By placing them in the same category as slaves and horses, Vives reveals the subordinate role he assigns women in the conjugal life. However, such an analogy may actually represent an *elevation* of a woman's social status by sixteenth-century standards. Vives reasons that if slaves and horses are given such a great deal of consideration at the time of purchase, one should pay at least equal attention to a potential wife, since she represents a lifelong companion.[32] This reasoning rests on the assumption that wives are given less consideration than slaves and horses, leading him to recommend that wives be scrutinized at the time of "purchase." If it is better to see an uncovered horse before purchase, he claims, then it is better to examine a potential wife with as little adornment as possible—hence the warning against deception exemplified by the "costra blanca" or powder she wears. By this definition, women literally belong to a "marriage market" where men represent the exclusive buyers.

De officio mariti, Vives's conduct manual directed to husbands, elaborates the analogy between women and horses that *The Education* introduces:

> ¿Pensamos, quizá, que se necesita maestría mayor para gobernar a una mujer que a un caballo coceador y arisco? El caballo, si no quiere sufrir jinete, hace

uso de su fuerza; pero es domado y señoreado por otra fuerza y por otra destreza, por manera que el caballo más robusto y batallador queda reducido a tal impotencia como si fuera un pollino recién nacido. . . . Y es que el hombre usa de la fuerza, del arte, de la astucia y del engaño.[33]

[Do we perhaps believe that greater skill is needed to govern a woman than a wild, bucking horse? If the horse does not want to suffer the rider, it will make use of force, but if it is tamed and controlled with force and skill even the strongest and fiercest horse will be reduced to such impotence as a newly born colt. . . . And this because man uses force, art, cunning and deception.]

Before reaching the conclusion that wild women, like untamed horses, must be dominated by brute strength, cunning and deception, Vives laments the popularity of books on horse husbandry, a subject he deems much less worthy than his own guide to a husband's duties. Vives points out that a wife deserves greater attention than she has received in the past, but as noble as this objective may appear, it is difficult to dismiss the absolute submission to which he reduces a wife in both *The Education* and *De officio mariti*. According to these texts, she must be "reduced to impotence," that is, she must submit all her power, all *potencia* to her husband, in order to successfully fulfill her role as a wife. A wife's role is therefore limited to strict obedience of her husband's will that is imposed on her by any means necessary. Marriage and its rites, by this definition, "*consecrate* force and violent forms of the appropriation of women and goods."[34]

It is also striking that *De officio mariti* should encourage deception as a means of achieving a wife's total submission, given the lengthy denouncement of cosmetics as instruments of falsehood. Deception, *De officio mariti* suggests, is permissible when a husband's exclusive privilege over his wife is at stake. Such a conclusion makes it difficult to affirm with Marcel Bataillon that Vives elevates women to the same intellectual level as men or that he treats them with "humana y amistosa comprensión" (humane and friendly understanding).[35] Rather, Vives's conclusions suggest a double standard in the precepts he directs to his readers. *De officio mariti* permits a husband to coerce a potentially subversive wife through deceit and even brute strength if necessary, while *The Education* strictly prohibits a wife from resorting to such strategies.

Given the heavy demands Vives places on a wife in the conjugal relation, one might ask what requirements he places on husbands. *The Education* proposes an ideal husband and details the specific professional, economic, and physical attributes a husband should possess. He should not be a pirate, pimp, or scoundrel. Other disreputable professions include executioners, mercenary soldiers, and innkeepers.[36] He should neither boast an inordinate amount of wealth nor be desperately poor, and he should be healthy and free of any hereditary diseases. He should be of at least marrying age but not too old to carry out his "conjugal duties."[37] Finally, a potential husband should not be pronouncedly unattractive in terms of physical beauty: "La fealdad no debe impedir el matrimonio, si no faltara todo lo demás, a menos que sea pronunciadísima y monstruosa" (ugliness should not be an impediment to marriage if the other qualities are not missing, unless it is truly horrendous and abominable).[38] Despite the specificity of these recommendations, however, Vives himself recognizes their limits:

> Con todo, y a pesar de todo lo dicho, ya más arriba insinué que el más vigilante cuidado y la diligencia más sagaz deben consagrarse a la índole, carácter y costumbres del marido que se busca. Es el único criterio con que debe el hombre estudiarse; ésta es única medida de estimación. Ni en la parte física ni en la fortuna hay elemento alguno del cual pueda formarse juicio seguro de un hombre: ni las riquezas, ni las posesiones, ni el abolengo, ni el poder, ni la influencia, ni la dignidad, ni las clientelas, ni belleza, ni salud, ni edad, ni entereza, ni prestancia, ni las contrarias cualidades; nada sin excepción, fuera del ingenio, en quien tienen su asiento la agudeza, la ambición, las virtudes, o en su defecto, el embotamiento, la rustiquez, los vicios.[39]

> [The greatest care and consideration, as I said previously, must be given to the future husband's character and morals. This is the one criterion we should use. On this we must base our judgment of a man. There is nothing in physical attributes or material well-being that can provide us with a sure estimation of a man: not riches, possessions, race, power, influence, dignity, entourage, beauty, health, age, soundness of body, stature, nor their opposites—nothing, in a word, but his character, in which are to be found intelligence, learning, and virtues, or their opposites: dullness, ignorance, and vice.][40]

According to this passage, the exterior signs of a man's worth do little to foretell his capacity to be a good husband. Vives recognizes the limits of outward displays of power, since such displays do not necessarily correspond to a person's present or potential ability to conform to the ethical standards he espouses. Power, wealth, and beauty are but trivial values next that of intelligence and a proven track record of good behavior. This passage is an eloquent expression of Vives's resistance to the prevailing attitude in Spain, where the importance of social standing and caste purity in both public and private human relations is difficult to exaggerate. Moreover, this passage softens the otherwise imperative tone of *The Education* and takes into account the unpredictability of human nature. It implies that certain precautions can be taken to ensure a better "match" although there is no guarantee that such a marriage will be successful. And yet, the exceptions Vives makes for men to qualify for marriage are not equally applied to women who must not only *be* chaste, but also *appear* chaste under all circumstances in order to retain an impeccable reputation: "A la pudicia cristiana no le basta con ser, sino también con parecer" (It is not enough for Christian modesty that it exist, but also that it appear so).[41] It is possible that "ser" (being) and "parecer" (appearing) are synonymous when referring to questions of feminine virtue in *The Education*, since collapsing the two terms enables greater control of women's behavior.

In *The Education*'s recommendation for a husband, Vives makes a claim for marriage that is related to human unpredictability, that is, marriage's presumed capacity for transformation. A scoundrel may be reformed and become a perfect gentleman by virtue of a good marriage.[42] Vives cites a case in which the young women of a Spanish village reformed the entire population of indolent young men by refusing them any "favors" until they had become "varones sesudos y duchos en la administración pública y privada" (men of great sagacity, skilled in public and private administration).[43] Despite such anecdotal evidence, Vives recognizes, not without bitterness, how the ideal he proposes conflicts with the reality he perceives. He goes to great lengths to deplore certain women's predilection for derelict young men who are masters of the art of seduction, but novices in "sage's studies."[44] The pitch of Vives's rhetoric reaches some of its highest points in a series of rhetorical questions directed to willing victims of male seduction:

> ¿Qué tratará, qué le dirá el marido estúpido, ignorante radical de toda cosa? ¿Qué cruz no será oír el rebuzno perpetuo de un asno? . . . considera, por otra parte, qué sabroso platicar con un marido ilustrado y prudente, puesto que no es posible hallar concierto más suave que la comunicación con un hombre así, y tanto más si está dotado de facundia."[45]

> [What would such a dolt, totally ignorant of everything, talk about? What a torture it will be to hear the ass constantly braying. . . . Consider, on the other hand, what conversations you will enjoy with a gifted and prudent man, such that no sweeter harmony could be found than the speech of this man, and all the more if added to that is the gift of eloquence.][46]

The overtly critical tone when referring to the husband who is "radically" ignorant and incapable of sustaining an intelligent conversation as an "ass" suggests the personal stakes involved in Vives's guide to the married life. His own pursuit of erudition would automatically qualify him as an ideal husband by his standards. The conjugal bond Vives proposes to his reader thus conforms to a vision whereby the ideal woman would desire him, the ideal man. While exempt of all the strategies of seduction employed by those "muchachos entregados a juegos," Vives's text may be read as an elaborate proposal, that is, he indirectly proposes *himself* as the embodiment of those qualities to which a woman should aspire.[47] It is striking that such a proposal should be couched in language that simultaneously sermonizes and instructs the reader.

While Vives expresses those qualities he finds most attractive in a woman, according to his own prescription, women should never articulate their own preferences, even when considering a lifetime companion.[48] *The Education* places the selection of a husband in the parents' hands, and even they should not betray excessive enthusiasm in their pursuit of an appropriate mate. Questions of consent would appear to be foregone conclusions if we consider the following case that Vives offers his reader as exemplary:

> Oigamos ahora cómo dice que recibió a los maridos que sus padres le entregaron: "Consentí" dijo, "en recibir al varón con temor vuestro, no con deseo mío." La doncella, pues, mientras sus padres andan ocupados en aquel negocio, ayúdeles con ruegos y oraciones.[49]

> [Let us hear how she says she received the men who were given to her by her parents: "I have consented to take a man out of respect for you, not because of my desire." Therefore, when her parents are engaged in these considerations, the young girl should help them by her prayers and supplications.][50]

In short, the rules of consent are not violated if it is assumed beforehand that a young woman does not possess authority and is therefore incapable of consenting to a vow of marriage.[51] Vives's insistence on this point reveals that he recognizes a woman's capacity to escape parental authority, although he clearly disapproves of such acts of defiance.

According to Vives, the ideal wife is one who lacks the ability to articulate her own, individual desires, and as such, he assigns very little value to a woman's speech, as illustrated in the first book of *The Education* devoted to a young girl's education: "Del bien hablar no tengo ningún cuidado; no lo necesita la mujer; lo que la mujer necesita es probidad y cordura; ni parece mal en la mujer el silencio" (I am not at all concerned with eloquence. A woman has no need for that; she needs rectitude and wisdom).[52] Vives advances a detailed plan of study that includes reading, but as this passage makes explicit, a woman's right to self-determination is inscribed within extremely limited bounds. While a woman may possess the ability to understand language, she is discouraged from developing the rhetorical tools that would permit her to employ language in any effective manner. Vives's text thus inscribes itself within a canonical tradition and commonplace of the period whereby women's active participation in the public sphere is prohibited. Not only should women remain silent, they should not in any way betray their thoughts through paralinguistic devices such as facial gestures or body language: "ni por señas ni por palabras" (with neither signs nor words).[53] Such a recommendation would be radically reversed by the exigencies of the dramatic genre that communicates precisely by means of such gestures.

Nonetheless, Vives does not subject women to abject ignorance, but defends their education, specifically a moral education:

> Y pues qué: ¿quieres que tu hija sepa al dedillo el mal y esté ayuna del bien? ¡Sabrá lo que encamina al crimen e ignorará lo que aparta del crimen? ¿Tan inicuo concepto tienes de la ciencia del bien que imaginas que va a serle nociva, si no le es nociva la ciencia del mal?[54]

> [What then? Do you wish your daughter to have knowledge of evil and be ignorant of good? Will she therefore comprehend things that lead to wickedness and be ignorant of things that lead us away from wickedness? Do you have such a prejudiced view of the knowledge of good that you deem it to be harmful while the knowledge of evil is not harmful?][55]

This passage underscores Vives's faith in the powers of learning that in turn lead to greater moral judgment regardless of the student's gender. Vives thus advocates an education where ethical understanding represents the ideal to which both men and women must aspire. Vives's ethical code for women in particular may stand in direct contradiction to her exercise of power, but it does not exclude her from exercising her moral judgment. This view of education, however, raises a series of difficulties. If women are forbidden from articulating their desires, how are they expected to defend themselves in situations of ambiguous morality? Is silence the only strategy available to women in defense of their virtue? Is such a strategy effective? The inherent contradictions and paradoxes of the moral code Vives espouses are not resolved in his text, nor would they necessarily be resolved in the dramatic works to follow. However, the "muchachos entregados a juegos," as well as the desirous, willful women Vives denounces would be given considerably more freedom of expression on the stage. And more often than not, these protagonists of the Spanish stage would directly confront the authority condemning them to silence.

The following passage from Juan Luis Vives's guide for husbands, *Deberes del marido* (*The Duties of a Husband*) re-creates the young Don Juans who engage a potential spouse with loving words and promises:

> No quisiera que contrajeras matrimonio con aquella con quien trataste demasi-ado de amores y a quien halagaste, lisonjeaste y serviste, llamándola "dueño mío", "vida mía", "luz de mis ojos", u otras cosas por el estilo que suele imaginar el amor necio e impertinente, a riesgo de fomentar la impiedad respecto a Dios, último fin de todas nuestras aspiraciones. Esa solicitud tuya trae aparejado tu rebajamiento a los ojos de la mujer, de tal suerte, que después quiere dominarte y se le hace muy cuesta arriba servir a quien en ciertos días le persuadía de su sumisión y le prometía cumplir sus más insignificantes deseos, por muchos peligros y dificultades que su realización ofrecía. De aquí el adagio: "quien casa por amores, malos días ha y buenas noches." Deseara yo que la llama que arde antes del matrimonio y se apaga apenas llega éste, encendiérase y permaneciera pura y viva después de efectuado.[56]

> [I would not like for you to contract marriage with a woman with whom you spoke too much of love and whom you praised, flattered and waited upon, calling her "my lady," "my life," "light of my eyes," and other such things that foolish and impertinent love imagines at the risk of encouraging irreverence in God, the end of all our aspirations. Your devotion brings with it your dis-grace in the eyes of the woman who afterwards wants to control you. It is an uphill battle to serve one who only a few days before was persuaded of your submission and whom you promised to realize her most insignificant desires, however dangerous and difficult they might be. Thus the proverb, "whoever marries for love, suffers during the day and has good nights." I want the flame that burns before marriage and is extinguished soon after, to remain pure and alive afterward.]

Here Vives dreams of an ideal marriage where a flame of "pure," chaste love might burn forever, but censures all those verbal sparks that might inflame carnal desire. This ideal excludes all those amorous expressions commonly associated with courtship on the grounds that they are impious and, more significantly, make a woman's later submission considerably more difficult. By this definition, the conjugal bond cannot be constituted by a promise to fulfill a woman's every whim, when a wife must presumably love, honor and most of all, obey her husband. But Vives's very insistence on a wife's submission, as well as his continual prohibitions and condemnations of all expressions of carnal desire, reveal the imperfections of the ideal he proposes. His conception of the conjugal bond excludes the ritual of courtship and thus excludes all terms of endearment and affection. How one consents to a bond that is indissoluble without showing the slightest inclination toward that very bond is, indeed, an engaging question. Although the *Siglo de Oro* dramatists would certainly show greater indulgence toward expressions of carnal desire, we may ask to what degree they share Vives's preoccupations with the institution of marriage.

Luis de León's Version of the Perfect Wife

Luis de León's treatise on marriage, *La perfecta casada* (*The Perfect Wife*), permits us to narrow the chronological gap separating Juan Luis Vives's *The Education* (1523) from the seventeenth-century Spanish dramas. Not only does *La perfecta casada* serve as a bridge connecting Juan Luis Vives to the Baroque playwrights; it also brings the reader closer to the Spanish cultural context of the later sixteenth century that had changed significantly since the publication of *The Education of the Christian Woman*.[57] Although Fray Luis was not compelled to live in exile, as was Vives, he was profoundly engaged in the ideological conflicts of his time.[58] An increased suspicion and intolerance of religious practices and intellectual endeavors deemed unorthodox by the Inquisition, exemplifies the second half of the sixteenth century and gives rise to the cultivation of mystical thought by such illustrious figures as Santa Teresa de Jesús and San Juan de la Cruz.[59] As one of Erasmus's intellectual heirs, Luis de León vigorously defended these endeavors and was unafraid to attack those who criticized him.[60] Fray Luis de León, like Vives before him, was subject to the Inquisition's persecution as a result of his *converso* origins and his polemic writings.[61]

One of the reasons that make *La perfecta casada* such an intriguing text is that it should revisit the subject of marriage at all. Most of the issues it raises, including marriage, chastity, and cosmetics were commonplace by the time of its publication in 1583; there is hardly a subject in Fray Luis's treatise that cannot be identified in Vives's *The Education of the Christian Woman* published sixty years earlier. The Council of Trent had already made its pronouncements on the sanctity of the conjugal bond, so to reiterate its conclusions as forcefully as does *La perfecta casada* might appear redundant. Therefore, to understand what makes *La perfecta casada* unique is not only a question of its subject matter *per se*, but also the circumstances in which it was written.

Fray Luis's earlier treatment of marriage in Solomon's *Song of Songs* (*Cantar de cantares*) sheds light on his later creation of *La perfecta casada*. One of the Inquisition's accusations leading to Fray Luis's arrest in 1572 involved his translation and commentary of the *Song of Songs* in 1561, "a passionate and tender surging which almost turns these pages into a real nuptial song."[62] Consisting of a dialogue between a husband and wife, Fray Luis's translation of this "nuptial song" is pertinent for its links to *La perfecta casada*. It is possible that *La perfecta casada*, written after his release from prison, responds to—and challenges—the authorities' exclusive control and suppression of Fray Luis's translation of the *Song of Songs*.[63]

Despite the significant differences distinguishing the *Song of Songs* from *La perfecta casada*—the first may be characterized as a love lyric, the second a didactic text—they share two defining characteristics rendering them subversive by post-Tridentine standards. The first consists of their point of departure in original Hebrew sources and the second has to do with their subsequent Spanish-language versions. These linguistic choices were fraught with risks as Klaus Reinhardt explains:

> Such a translation put into doubt the authority of the Latin Vulgate. As such, it is not surprising that ecclesiastic authorities did not look kindly upon various attempts to translate the Hebrew and Greek Bible again into Latin. . . . During the Protestant Reformation translations into Romance languages were still more suspicious than Latin translations. Several of the Spanish Inquisition's Indexes prohibited the translation of Biblical books into Romance languages. Fernando de Valdés's Index of 1559 prohibits complete or partial translations of the Bible into the Vulgate. . . . It is for this reason that during the second half of the sixteenth century we have very few Romance translations of the *Song of Songs*.[64]

Given the risks involved in translation, Fray Luis's works are not, therefore, strictly academic exercises performed in monastic isolation; rather, they engage his social and intellectual community in ways that would put into question their most orthodox convictions.[65] This engagement leads us to another significant parallel between the *Song of Songs* and *La perfecta casada*: in both cases, their intended readers were women.

Fray Luis's translations and commentaries of Hebrew texts put into question the Church's authority to control the circulation of information. His work on the *Song of Songs*, as well as that of the twenty Proverbs dedicated to wives in *La perfecta casada* render these texts accessible to a far wider public. In particular, they make their knowledge available to the women to whom they are dedicated. Specifically, Fray Luis directs his *Song of Songs* to his cousin Isabel Osorio, a nun in the convent of Sancti Spiritus in Salamanca, while he dedicates *La perfecta casada* to his recently married niece, María Varela Osorio.[66] In comparison to the Queen of Aragon to whom Vives dedicated his manual, neither Isabel nor María are distinguished by their elevated social status. In this sense, they are more representative of average, sixteenth-century Spanish women and of the limited alternatives available to them. This fact was not lost on the Inquisition that duly documented the unsanctioned circulation of the *Song of Songs*: "pareçe no se devia permitir que este anduviese en romance *specialmente en manos de mugeres* a quien pareçe ser scripta esta sposiçion" (It seems that this [text] should not have been permitted to circulate in romance, *especially in the hands of a woman* for whom this piece seems to have been written).[67] By means of Fray Luis's work, direct knowledge of the Bible is no longer limited to those few, exceptional women who read Latin. In fact, Fray Luis facilitates access to some of the most highly censored portions of the Bible. The *Cantar* whose lesson Fray Luis confesses "difficultosa a todos y peligrosa alos mançebos y alos que aun no estan muy adelantados y muy firmes en la virtud" (difficult for everyone, dangerous for boys, and for those who do not have a developed and steadfast sense of virtue), was, after his translation, in the hands of a nun.[68] No longer are women subject to abject ignorance of matters directly concerning them.

Fray Luis's translation of a Hebrew text whose intended reader was a woman undoubtedly represented a challenge to the Inquisition's authority. But it was the expression of erotic desire in the *Cantar* that made it especially unpalatable for Fray Luis's most prudish readers. According to Jorge Guillén, "hubo quien leyó 'hasta media plana pequeña' y no pudo seguir adelante."[69] The specific accusation against Fray Luis's *Cantar* by the Holy Office reads as follows:

> Ytenque el dicho Fray Luys de Leon, confirmando los dichos herrores, ha dicho afirmado que los *Cantares de Salomón* eran *carmen amatorium ad suam uxorem* y profanando los dichos *Cantares* los traduxero en lengua bulgar, y estan y andan en poder de muchas personas, a quienes el los dio, y de otras en la dicha lengua de romançe.[70]

> [And said Fray Luis de Leon, having affirmed said errors, has affirmed that the *Song of Solomon* was a *carmen amatorium ad suam uxorem*. And he profaned said *Song* by translating it into the vulgate, and it is and continues to be in hands of many people to whom he gave these verses, as well as others in the said romance language.]

According to this charge, to claim the *Cantar de los cantares* represents a love song for one's spouse was as serious a transgression as "profaning" these verses by translating them into the vernacular. The Inquisition itself does not even name the presumed crime in Spanish, but instead identifies what it considers blasphemous in Latin (*carmen amatorium ad suam uxorem*). This Latin reference to a "love song for one's wife" calls attention to one of the main contradictions of censorship: it reveals more than it conceals in its attempt to repress its subject.

By directing attention to marriage as a possible sight of erotic desire in the *Cantar*, Fray Luis breaks a long-standing literary tradition excluding such expressions for one's spouse. Although Fray Luis defended himself by claiming that the *Cantar* deals with spiritual rather than carnal love, a distinct eroticism pervades the entire work.[71] When the Wife initiates the *Cantar* with the verse, "Beseme de besos de su boca, que buenos son tus amores más que el vino" (Let him kiss me with the kisses of his mouth, for your love is better than wine), Fray Luis does not condemn her for expressing sensuous desire:

> Y no ay que pedille vergüença eneste caso que el mirar en eros achaques es de flaqueza de afición. Que el amor grande y verdadero rompe con todo, y muestase tan razonable y conforme al entendimiento del que ama que no le da lugar imaginar que a nadie le puede parecer otra cosa.[72]

> [And she does not need to be ashamed in this case, for to see harm in Eros constitutes weak devotion. A great and true love disregards everything and shows itself to be so reasonable and in agreement with a lover's understanding, that it cannot imagine anyone would see it otherwise.]

According to this passage, the Wife's expression of desire bespeaks an overwhelming passion for her husband. Missing from this commentary are references to "chaste" marriage or admonisments of silence, so often prescribed by the conduct manuals. Instead, Fray Luis's admission of the Wife's "great love" represents a significant shift from the predominant conception of her role in marriage. In the *Cantar* she is not compelled to repress her desire; rather, the lyric provides a context in which desire is given meaning, defined here as the longing one feels in the absence of the beloved. By the same token, Fray Luis may have indirectly contributed to endowing marriage with erotic qualities far more attractive to its participants than any social obligation. Few, if any, of the conduct manuals offer as persuasive an argument to join in wedlock. Significantly, this expression of tolerance is absent from his Latin re-edition of the *Cantar* of 1580, written after his trial, and according to Fray Luis, written against his will.[73]

In Fray Luis's prologue, he defines the *Cantar* as *una égloga pastoril* (a pastoral eclogue) in which a shepherd and his wife engage in dialogue.[74] These figures, he claims, are allegorical representations of Christ and his bride, the Church.[75] This explanation might appear to dismiss any interpretations of the *Cantar* in which carnal desire finds a voice. Despite this disclaimer, however, Fray Luis insists that his commentary in the *Cantar* will dwell on its literal, "superficial" meaning, as if deciphering the writing on the bark of a tree: "Solamente trabajare en declarar la corteza de la letra asy llanamente *como si eneste libro no vuiera otro mayor secreto* del que muestran aquellas palabras desnudas y al parecer dichas y respondidas entre Solomon y su esposa" (I will only work to reveal the surface of the word as plainly *as if there were no greater secret* than that shown by the naked word and which seems to be stated and exchanged between Solomon and his wife).[76] Paradoxically, it is this literal interpretation of the *Cantar* that lays bare the private parts of the spouse's dialogue. A verse such as "Beseme de besos de su boca" refers to the beloved's kisses which Fray Luis represents as the superlative expression of sensual pleasure and desire: "aqui es el desear tanto y deleitarse los que se aman." (here is the desire and pleasure of those who love each other).[77] Fray Luis thus invokes the allegorical basis of the *Cantar* only to disregard it.

By defining the *Cantar* as a pastoral eclogue, Fray Luis provides a literary framework that accomplishes at least two interrelated objectives. First of all, the pastoral situates the abstract concept of spiritual experience within familiar literary territory. To render this spiritual experience accessible to the reader constitutes an objective consonant with Fray Luis's lifelong dedication to facilitating knowledge through translation and commentary. Secondly, the pastoral provides a space where the absence of social restraints permits the expression of erotic desire. However, it is not irrelevant that desire in the *Cantar* derives from a couple bound by the *social* institution of marriage. This intersection of the pastoral and the social enables the married couple to behave according to the poetic conventions of the pastoral, that is, as lovers ostensibly unbound by the Church or State. Although it may be argued that the conjunction of erotic and conjugal love is made possible only because it takes place within the imaginative realm of the pastoral, Fray Luis's representation of marriage stands in direct contrast to the dominant moral codes upheld by writers such as Vives. The two distinct conceptions of marriage—one that includes erotic desire and another that represses it—are only reconciled with difficulty.

After Fray Luis's four-year imprisonment by the Inquisition from 1572 to 1576, he returns to the subject of marriage in *La perfecta casada*, a text dedicated to women who take up this "state" or *estado*. Unlike the *Cantar*, *La perfecta casada* is marked by a decidedly didactic tone that shares a great deal with the conduct manuals preceding it, particularly *The Education*. Here again are the recommendations regarding chastity—"el ser y la substancia de la casada" (a wife's being and substance)—as well as praise for marriage's sacramental status, "Sacramento santísimo del lazo de amor" (Most holy sacrament of love's bonds). Vives's injunctions against novels of chivalry and the love lyric are also present in *La perfecta casada*:

> que las escusen y libren del leer en los libros de caballerías, y del traer el soneto y la canción en el seno, y del billete, y del donaire de los recados, y del terrero, y del sarao, y de cient cosas deste jaez, aunque nunca las hagan.

> [they will excuse and pardon their reading books of chivalry, and having sonnets and song-sheets tucked into their bosoms, and exchanging love notes, and their flirtations and dances and many other things of this ilk in which they may or may not have engaged.][78]

Similarly, there is a great deal of emphasis on the preservation and development of domestic economy. The conservation of material resources reflects an overall preoccupation consonant with Spain's worsening economic conditions in the second half of the sixteenth century.[79] Despite this economic crisis, however, the means by which women are to achieve greater prosperity remain essentially the same. The advice and admonishments Fray Luis offers his readers echoes that of his predecessors: wives must be resourceful, not incur unnecessary expense, and avoid the ostentatious display of wealth.

Above all, women are relegated to a private, domestic sphere where they are to remain if they are to successfully fulfill their obligations as defined by Fray Luis's text. These obligations are defined in negative terms throughout *La perfecta casada*, that is, rather than instruct them as to how and when to accomplish their duties, women are warned against what they should *not* do:

> Y demás desto, si la casada no trabaja ni se ocupa en lo que pertenece a su casa, ¿qué otros estudios o negocios tiene en que se ocupar? Forzado es que, si no trata de sus oficios, emplee su vida en los oficios ajenos, y que dé en ser ventanera, visitadora, callejera, amiga de fiestas, enemiga de su rincón, de su casa olvidada y de las casas ajenas curiosa, pesquisidora de cuanto pasa, y aun de lo que no pasa inventora, parlera y chismosa, de pleitos revolvedora, jugadora también, y dada del todo a la risa y a la conversación y al palacio, con lo demás por ordinaria consecuencia se sigue y se calla aquí agora, por ser cosa manifiesta y notoria.

> [And furthermore, if the married woman does not work at and occupy herself with that which is connected with the house, what other business is there for her to occupy herself with? If she does not deal with her tasks, it is inevitable that she will employ her time in other people's tasks and that she will be always at the windows, or out visiting, or walking the streets, or frequenting different gatherings, neglecting her own corner and ignoring her house but noseying

into other people's business, prying into what has happened and even invent-
ing things which have not, chattering and gossiping, stirring up trouble, gambling even, and completely given over to laughter and conversation and the
court with all that it ordinarily entails and which we do not need to mention
here because it is so evident and well known.][80]

This passage, ostensibly designed to satirize women's behavior, produces
the portrait of woman who takes great delight in crossing the line enclosing
her within the strict confines of her home. Neither passive nor reserved,
this woman represents everything the "perfect wife" is not. Ironically, this
diatribe against the socialite offers an alternative to the cloistered life Fray
Luis proposes. While the woman this passage describes possesses negative
qualities, it also assigns her an enormous, almost irrepressible energy to
transgress the social barriers that restrict her movement and public presence. Just as significantly, the means by which she accesses the world
outside her home are described in terms of her extraordinary verbal ability:
"parlera" (chatterbox), "dada del todo a la risa y a la conversación" (given
over to laughter and conversation). Recognizing this capacity for speech,
Fray Luis will later invoke the familiar arguments in favor of women's
silence. Despite the detailed portrait of a wife who neglects her duties in
favor of more pleasurable pursuits, this passage also "keeps silent" a reality
it claims is obvious to everyone. That is, such a portrait may reflect actual
women who were not compelled to follow the dictates of silence and obedience prescribed by the moralists.

Unlike previous conduct manuals, *La perfecta casada* focuses exclusively
on wives' roles, dispensing with instructions for finding a husband or advice
for the grieving widow. As its title indicates, *La perfecta casada* represents
more than a conduct manual—it proposes an ideal to which wife is expected
to aspire. Who is the "perfect wife" to which the title refers? The text does
not offer a concrete description of the model it proposes, but rather, assumes
the reader's ability to deduce this model according to its dictates; in other
words, it requires an imaginative leap from theory to practice on the part of
the reader. The text also requires that the reader extract a positive model
from the negative examples it provides. *La perfecta casada* therefore demands
an active rather than a passive approach on the part of the reader, although
the model it proposes is not necessarily accessible to all. Perfection belongs
to a category permanently beyond the reach of the reader, and as such, contradicts the social realities that impede its realization. As a result, a constant
tension between the ideal and the real traverses *La perfecta casada*. Nonetheless, the prologue suggests a place where one might locate the perfection it
advocates:

Dios, por la boca de Salomón, por unas mismas palabras hace dos cosas. Lo uno, instruye y ordena las costumbres, lo otro profetiza misterios secretos. Las costumbres que ordena, son de la casada; los misterios que profetiza son el ingenio, y las condiciones que había de poner su Iglesia, de quien habla *como en figura de una mujer de su casa*.

[God through Solomon's lips, does two things through the same words: one, He teaches and sets out ways of behaving; two, He prophesies deep mysteries. The ways of behaving he sets out are those of the wife; the mysteries he prophesies are the nature and conditions He was to infuse in His church, of which He speaks *in the form of a married woman in the home*.][81]

Solomon's proverbs not only instruct wives, but also "prophesy mysterious secrets" pertaining to the Church that he allegorically represents as "una mujer de su casa." The Church, therefore, represents the ultimate wife, wedded to Christ, the ultimate husband. This marriage is not only of a spiritual order, but also possesses a metaphorical dimension; consequently, wifely perfection is not only a moral, religious ideal, but also a literary construct. In other words, the perfect wife is a figment of Fray Luis's poetic imagination.

The ideal of wifely perfection stands in stark contrast to Fray Luis's metaphor of marriage as a long and arduous journey:

Y, como suelen los que han hecho alguna larga navegación o los que han peregrinado por lugares estraños, que a sus amigos, los que quieren emprender la misma navegación y camino, antes que lo comiencen y antes que partan de sus casas, con diligencia y cuidado les dicen menudamente los lugares por donde han de pasar, y las cosas de que se han de guardar, y los aperciben de todo aquello que entienden les será necesario, así yo, en esta jornada que tiene Vuestra Merced comenzada, le enseñaré, no lo que me enseñó a mí la experiencia pasada, porque es ajena de mi profesión, sino lo que he aprendido en las Sagradas Letras, que es enseñanza del Espíritu Sancto.

[And as happens with those who have undertaken a long sea voyage or travelled through strange lands who, when their friends wish to travel and undertake a similar voyage, tell them with diligence and care the details of the places through which they have to pass and advise them about everything they think they will need, so I will teach you, in this journey you have embarked upon, not what past experience taught me, for such experience is foreign to my profession, but that which I have learned from the Sacred Scriptures, which is the teaching of the Holy Spirit.][82]

In this passage, the narrative voice authorizes itself to speak on a subject of which it claims no personal experience. Despite this lack of authority, the narrator offers advice just as he would to a friend about to embark on a long trip or pilgrimage. The vacillation between these metaphors of marriage—trip or pilgrmage—may not be insignificant, for the latter has resonances recalling unions of a more spiritual sort, such as that of Christ and the Church described in the *Cantar*. On the other hand, the nautical metaphor invariably recalls the period of intense overseas exploration and colonization in which Fray Luis lived. According to Elias L. Rivers, "the predominant meaning of the sea in his poetry is emblematic or allegorical, the sea is an uncertain path of commercial greed."[83] If this is indeed the case, then *La perfecta casada* offers contrasting metaphors of marriage; one as spiritual union and the other as an economic and political union. The predominance of metaphors of exploration and exploitation in *La perfecta casada* suggest that the political and economic dimensions of the institution of marriage prevail over those of the spiritual in this treatise. This pragmatic vision of marriage is consonant with the sense of disenchantment or *desencanto* characterizing Spain at the close of the sixteenth century.

Solomon's proverbs, on which Fray Luis bases *La perfecta casada*, characterizes the good wife as "a ship laden with merchandise." Fray Luis preserves and elaborates Solomon's original metaphor according to his own, historical paradigm:

Y, como el que navega a las Indias, de las agujas que lleva, y de los alfileres, y de otras cosas de aqueste jaez, que acá valen poco y los indios lo estiman en mucho, trae rico oro y piedras preciosas, así esta nave que vamos pintando ha de convertir en riqueza lo que pareciere más desechado, y convertirlo sin parecer que hace algo en ello, sino con tomarlo en la mano y tocarlo, como hace la nave, que sin parecer que se menesa, nunca descansa, y cuando los otros duermen, navega ella y acrecienta con sólo mudar el aire el valor de lo que recibe . . . y cuasi sin sentir cómo o de qué manera, se hace rica.

[And just as the person who sails to the Indies comes back with valuable gold and precious stones in place of the needles and pins and other items of this sort which he has taken there and which are of little worth here but highly valued by the Indians, so this ship we are describing must turn into something valuable that which may seem to be of least worth, and transform it without appearing to be doing anything to it, simply by taking hold of it and touching it, just as the ship which, without appearing to move, is never motionless, and when others are sleeping, it is sailing and, through a mere change of wind, it enhances the value of what it has received . . . and almost without knowing by what manner or means, she becomes rich.][84]

This nautical metaphor simplifies the inherent difficulties and ethical conflicts involved in producing and protecting material wealth in sixteenth-century Spain. If, with pins and needles, a wife is expected to stitch and sew together the fabric of her home's economy, she must do so at considerable expense to herself. She must renounce the public space traversed daily by the merchant and explorer who goes into the world to buy and sell his wares. Nevertheless, this image of the wife as ship places her on the side of the merchant, rather than on the side of the indigenous "other" who is the actual source of goods sought after by the Spaniards during this period.

In the journey a woman undertakes when she contracts marriage, the narrator characterizes the places she will visit as "strange" ("lugares estraños"). Although the narrator admits no direct knowledge of these places, he nevertheless claims to have *access* to the subject of marriage by means of biblical teachings. Fray Luis had previously visited the "place" of marriage in the *Cantar*, but the discursive framework of *La perfecta casada* is decidedly different. No longer does marriage inhabit an idyllic, pastoral world; rather, it is confronted by the exigencies of political, religious, and economic upheaval to which Fray Luis himself was subjected. Had Fray Luis never written his translation and commentary on the *Cantar*, *La perfecta casada* might appear to be the logical continuation of conduct manuals designed to control women's behavior. However, in the wider context of his other works, *La perfecta casada* takes on greater significance. The moral values his treatise espouses may conform in large part to those of its predecessors, but Fray Luis never renounces his right to access the "strange place" of marriage for which he was so severely punished by the Inquisition.

In this regard, the introductory words to the Latin re-edition of the *Cantar* written after Fray Luis's release from prison are revealing: "juzgaba ciertamente que en este nuestro tiempo la tarea de escribir, no solo para los que editan tantos nuevos libros sino velan y atienden a recoger los escritos buenos de otros, no es muy útil para los demás y es demasiado peligrosa para los que escriben" (I truly believed that in our day the task of writing, not only for those who edit so many new books, but also for those who are vigilant and take care to gather good writings from others, is not very useful and is too dangerous for those who write).[85] The weary tone of these words puts into question Fray Luis's hermeneutic enterprise, but the passage also reveals a sense of anxiety concerning the risks one assumes when writing a controversial or altogether censored subject. Fray Luis re-edits the polemical work of his youth, but its Latin renders it less accessible to the larger, female readership for which it was originally intended. This re-edition illustrates the complex negotiations involved in approaching the subject of marriage in sixteenth-century Spain. Inquisitorial authority circumscribed the topic within extremely narrow terms in order to ensure control over sexuality, especially female sexuality. Although the precepts of *La perfecta casada* conform to and uphold these terms, the fact that he returns to the subject of marriage—a subject for which he had been persecuted—perhaps should not be discounted.

Notes

1. Translations of *Instrucción* de la mujer cristiana first appear in German (1524), English (1529), French (1543), and Italian (1561). The English translation suggests its positive reception, at least on the part of the translator Richard Hyrde, who changes the title substantially: A *very fruitefull and pleasant booke called the instructio[n] of a Christen woma[n]*).

2. According to Charles Fantazzi, "whatever its failings, the *De institutione* enjoyed an enormous popularity and was generally regarded as the most authoritative statement on this subject throughout the sixteenth century, especially in England, where it found favor with Catholics and Protestants alike. There can be no denying that merely by attaching such importance to the education of women, Vives laid the groundwork for the Elizabethan age of the cultured woman. The impact of his treatise, positive and negative, must be taken into account in any chronicling of the emergence of the other voice in early modern Europe." In Vives, *The Education of a Christian Woman*, 3.

3. Ibid., 50.

4. This defense appears later under the title of *Encomium matrimonii* and finally in *De conscribendis epistolis*. In Spain, Francesc Eiximinis (1330/35–1409), Vicente Ferrer (1350–1419), and Jaime Roig ([?]–1478) preceded Vives as concerns the subject of women's education. Roig's *Spill* narrates the story of a man who, after four broken marriages, has a dream in which King Solomon warns him against contracting a fifth marriage. Narrated in the first person, *Spill's* unrestrained misogyny, as well as King Solomon's imaginary intervention, distinguishes it from Vives's work. Eiximinis's *Lo libre de les dones*, on the other hand, is much closer in style and tone to *The Education* and devotes attention to many of the same topics, including marriage and women's education.

5. See Telle, *Érasme de Rotterdam et le septième sacrement: étude d'evangélisme matrimonial au XVI siècle et contribution a la biographie intellectuelle d'Érasme*, 315.

6. Vives, *Obras completas*, 1072.

7. Vives, *The Education of a Christian Woman*, 327.

8. Erasmus, *Collected Works of Erasmus*, 137.

9. Vives, *Obras completas*, 1073.

10. Erasmus, *Collected Works of Erasmus*, 134.

11. Ibid.

12. Vives, *Obras completas*, 1073.

13. Although *The Education* was originally written in Latin, Juan Justiniano translated it into Spanish soon after its first publication and received a wider dissemination as a consequence of this translation. Other translations include Richard Hyrde's translation originally published in London and titled *A very frutefull and pleasant boke callyd The Instruction of a Christian Woman* (1529); Pierre de Changy's French translation, *Livre très bon, plaisant et salutaire de l'Institution de la femme chretienne en son enfance, marriage et viduité, avec l'Office du Mary* (1542) which enjoyed twelve subsequent editions.

14. Vives, *Obras completas*, 989–90.

15. For an engaging account of these events see Mattingly, *Catherine of Aragon*.

16. Virginia Walcott Beauchamp *et al.* summarizes some of the principal critical oversights that Vives's biography has suffered: "Scholars . . . have been generally unaware of the life story of its author. Similarly, scholars focusing on the humanist thinker's life and times, or on his many influential philosophical and religious writings, have paid little attention to his work on women. Thus members of neither group appear to have recognized the conjoining of certain traumatic events in Vives's life with the creation of this extraordinary treatise." Vives, *The Instruction of a Christian Woman*, 15. Other critics to devote attention to *The Education* include Marcel Bataillon, Emilie Bergmann, Mary Elizabeth Perry, and Leo Esteban Mateo.

17. Jorge García Reyes, *El matrimonio de las minorías religiosas en el derecho español*, 96.

18. Pinta Llorente and Palacio y de Palacio, José María de, *Procesos inquisitoriales contra la familia judía de Juan Luis Vives*, 104.

19. José Ortega y Gasset's observations exemplify scholarly disregard for the circumstances of Vives's life: "bastan cuatro palabras: nació, estudió, escribió, murió" (four words suffice: he was born, studied, wrote, and died). Ortega y Gasset, *Vives-Goethe: Conferencias*, 72. While this reduction of his biography serves to emphasize Vives's dedication to a life of letters, it also reveals the degree to which scholarship has, until recently, eluded the very dramatic circumstances of his life. Ortega y Gasset's comment suggests that intellectual pursuits may be divorced from the political, religious, and social circumstances that produce them. His affirmation that Vives's life could be summarized in four words was prophetic for future studies on the sixteenth-century humanist, as scholarship repeatedly refused to recognize Vives's *converso* origins. In the only complete edition of Vives's work to date from 1947, we find the following claim in the introduction: "What does, in fact, deserve to be rejected instinctually until more authoritative proof than a simple suspicion based on the identity of a last name can offer, is Juan Luis Vives's presumed Jewish origin. It pains us greatly to see the most Christian of epigones of the Renaissance sullied, that is, author of *Meditations and Prayers, Mass of Christ's Sacred Labor*, and the fervent and hardened defender in *The Truth of the Christian Faith*, victorious vanquisher of Muslims and Jews." In Vives, *Obras completas*, 15. Such claims have undoubtedly done a great deal to impoverish the state of past and present scholarship on Vives and reveal

a great deal more about his biographer's anti-Semitism than Vives, who divulged very little of the circumstances that caused him to live in exile. However, this silence may in fact be an even clearer indication of the precarious circumstances of his existence and his attempts to protect his family that remained in Spain.

20. Ibid., 985–86.

21. Vives, *The Education of a Christian Woman*, 46.

22. Vives, *Obras completas*, 985.

23. Ibid., 1139–40; 1157–63.

24. Ibid., 988. Vives, *The Education of a Christian Woman*, 50.

25. Vives, *Obras completas*, 995; Vives, *The Education of a Christian Woman*, 62.

26. Vives, *Obras completas*, 1026.

27. Vives, *The Education of a Christian Woman*, 109.

28. "Las damas no desdigan de su nombre. / Y si mudaren traje, sea de modo / que pueda perdonarse, porque suele /el disfraz varonil agradar mucho" (May the ladies not betray their gender / and if they change costumes, may it be in such a way / that it can be forgiven / for a man's costume tends to be very pleasing). Lope de Vega's *Arte nuevo de escribir comedias en este tiempo* (*The New Art of Writing Plays in This Time*), lines 280–83.

29. Later in the century, the statutes regarding apparel instituted by Phillip II and in the next century by Phillip IV would echo Vives's own directives. These prohibited the use of certain garments, such as the elaborate white lace collars ("lechugilla") worn by the aristocracy or the whale ribs ("guardainfante") that supported wide, billowing skirts. Perhaps no other article of clothing and its subsequent prohibition caused more controversy in sixteenth-century Spain than the veil ("tapado de medio ojo"). Defourneaux, *La vida cotidiana en la España del siglo de oro*, 151–55.

30. Vives, *Obras completas*, 1016.

31. Vives, *The Education of a Christian Woman*, 96.

32. Vives, *Obras completas*, 1261.

33. Ibid.

34. Klapisch-Zuber, *Women, Family, and Ritual in Renaissance Italy*, 255.

35. Bataillon, *Erasmo y España*, 634.

36. Vives, *Obras completas*, 1060.

37. Ibid.

38. Ibid. English translation by Charles Fantazzi in Vives, *The Education of a Christian Woman*, 159.

39. Vives, *Obras completas*, 1061, emphasis added.

40. Vives, *The Education of a Christian Woman*, 159.

41. Vives, *Obras completas*, 1024; Vives, *The Education of a Christian Woman*, 106.

42. Vives, *Obras completas*, 1067.

43. Ibid., 1061–62; Vives, *The Education of a Christian Woman*, 163.

44. Vives, *Obras completas*, 1062–63.

45. Ibid., 1065.

46. Vives, *The Education of a Christian Woman*, 164–65.

47. Vives, *Obras completas*, 1062.

48. Ibid., 1069.

49. Ibid., 1059.

50. Vives, *The Education of a Christian Woman*, 156–57.

51. Esteban Mateo elaborates on the problem of consent: "It could not be any other way . . . as seen from the view that virginity 'does not know nor desire sexual union, nor does it even think of it . . .' The solution is a product of previous reasoning. If there is only pure love in the maiden and she has even transcended this love, if there is no freedom to know [the groom] beforehand, there is no choice whatsoever. The reasons offered as justification of such a measure matter little to us . . . 'How can a maiden enclosed within the walls of her home, know the character and the habits of a possible husband?' The last question verges on the cynical—but who locked her up in the first place?" Esteban Mateo, *Hombre-Mujer en Vives*, 138.

52. Vives, *Obras completas*, 1001; Vives, *The Education of a Christian Woman*, 71.

53. Vives, *Obras completas*, 1069.

54. Ibid., 996.

55. Vives, *The Education of a Christian Woman*, 64.

56. Vives, *Obras completas*, 1293.

57. Cristóbal Cuevas García's introduction to his edition of *De los nombres de Cristo* summarizes the changes Fray Luis experiences during his lifetime: "Born in the third decade of the century, the Augustinian received nearly all of his education during the Emperor's [Charles V] lifetime, but creates his oeuvre under Phillip II. His personality therefore straddles both Spains." León, *De los nombres de Cristo*, 22.

58. According to Manuel Durán, "Luis de León was able to teach his contemporaries not only through the example of his art but also by dint of his courageous life. As an *engaged* intellectual he took part in more than one battle of ideas. He may have forgiven his enemies—yet he never ceased thinking and writing what he thought. More than once his bravery verged on temerity. He won his battles and enjoyed letting his enemies know about his victory." Durán, *Luis de Léon*, 6.

59. Elliott, *Imperial Spain 1469–1716*, 244–45.

60. Bataillon, *Erasmo y España*, 763.

61. Ángel Alcalá provides an example of the way in which *converso* origins motivate the persecution of Fray Luis and his colleagues, Gaspar de Grajal and Martín Martínez de Cantalapiedra: "The three teachers from Salamanca shared another characteristic: their *converso* caste. The order of imprisonment signed by the dangerous inquisitor Diego González . . . could not be more explicit: 'Because Grajal and Fray Luis are notorious *conversos*, I believe they want nothing else but to obscure our Catholic faith and to turn against its law, and for this reason, it is my vote and belief that Fray Luis de Leon should be imprisoned and brought to the prisons of the Holy Office so that the prosecutor can follow this case.' There is no doubt that

suspicions of heterodoxy in the three cases were motivated by their Jewish origins. . . . Various phases of the three trials relay dozens of affirmations to this effect." Alcalá, "Pecularidad de las acusaciones a fray Luis en el marco del proceso a sus colegas salmantinos," 70.

62. Durán, *Luis de Léon*, 91. Other accusations against Fray Luis included his translations of the Bible, which put into question the authority of the Vulgate version. Ángel Alcalá summarizes Fray Luis's dedication to biblical hermeneutics: "His passion was the Bible and he did not miss the opportunity to take advantage of his professorship . . . to consider in an absolutely original way such delicate subjects as the transmission of Biblical texts, the 'authenticity' of the Latin Vulgate translation . . . and the value or utility of Jewish commentators in providing a literal understanding of the Old Testament. Alcalá, "Pecularidad de las acusaciones a fray Luis en el marco del proceso a sus colegas salmantinos," 69. The full documentation pertaining to Fray Luis's trial may be found in Alcalá's compilation of these materials in *Proceso inquisitorial de Fray Luis de León*.

63. Mar Martinez-Góngora suggests just such a possibility: "By means of the subject of women, the author gives free reign to his nonconformity with the social model at the end of the sixteenth century. To write about women in *La perfecta casada* is sometimes a pretext for Luis de Leon; it is the vehicle by which the writer criticizes contemporary Spanish society in a veiled but profound way." Martínez-Góngora, *Discursos sobre la mujer en el humanismo renacentista español*, 163.

64. Reinhardt, "Una exposición castellana del Cantar de los cantares, hasta ahora desconocida, atribuida a Fray Luis de León," 475.

65. In Fray Luis's defense, he describes, how copies of the *Cantar* were made without his knowledge: "Y acaecio que un fraile que tenia cargo de my celda, que se llama fray Diego de Leon, que agora está en la provincia de Aragon, hallando abierto un escritorio donde yo tenia dicho libro lo sacó con otros papeles y los trasladó sin sabello ny entendello yo, y de aquel tralado en poco meses, sin venir a my noticia, se multiplicaron tantos otros traslados que quando lo supe aunque desée y procuré recogello no me fue posible, y asi según e entendido se a derramado por muchas partes el dicho libro contra toda my voluntad" (And it so happened that a friar who was in charge of my cell and who is named Diego de Leon and now resides in the province of Aragon, found my desk open. There I had said book, and he took it and copied it without my knowlege or understanding. And within a few months and unbeknownst to me, the copies multiplied, and when I found out, I wanted and tried to get back the manuscript, but it was not possible. And this is how I know that my book has been widely circulated, entirely against my consent). Alcalá, *Proceso inquisitorial de Fray Luis de León*, 26–27. This passage does not deny responsibility for a text written against the Inquisition's prohibitions. Rather, it places emphasis on its circulation over which he claims no control. This defense permits Fray Luis to reverse the terms of his accusation in a very crucial manner; he reserves the right to access prohibited texts while reasserting his claim over his translation. Although the Inquisition absolved Fray Luis of most of the charges

against him, its final declarations regarding the translation of the *Cantar* suggests that it remained unconvinced of Fray Luis's defense.

66. According to Marcel Bataillon, the Inquisition condemned Fray Luis's translation of the *Cantar* precisely because it had been rendered for Isabel Osorio: "Uno de los capítulos de acusación de su primer proceso era que había traducido al castellano el *Cantar de los cantares* y que había comentado 'a lo divino' este canto de amor para la monja Isabel Osorio. Al transgredir la prohibición inquisitorial a favor de una religiosa entregada a la oración, había dado pruebas de la misma amplitud de miras que recomendaba en otro tiempo Carranza" (*Erasmo* 761).

67. Alcalá, *Proceso inquisitorial de Fray Luis de León*, 67. Emphasis added.

68. León, *Cantar de cantares de Salomón*, 46.

69. Quoted in León, *Cantar de cantares*, 144.

70. León, *Escritos desde la cárcel*, 435–36.

71. Mar Martínez-Góngora notes an exception to this rule: "Fray Luis translates the Hebrew word 'Zama' which literally refers to a woman's sex as well as to her hair . . . thus contradicting Saint's Jerome's 'official' translation. Fray Luis changes the translation because 'some little words that Saint Jerome used in his translation could be improved.'" Martínez-Góngora, *Discursos sobre la mujer en el humanismo renacentista español*, 167.

72. León, *Cantar de cantares de Salomón*, 60.

73. Fray Luis describes this coercion in his prologue to this edition: "lo hice coaccionanado en cierto modo, no siguiendo tanto mi opinión cuanto el parecer de los que me quieren bien . . . no niego que me ha sucedido, lo que debe sucederle a todos los que llevados más por la necesidad que el deseo escriben algo, que no están de acuerdo con muchas cosas de las que escriben. Estoy descontento conmigo en muchas cosas. Pues al estar obligado y ser llamado a otro lugar distinto del que desea, la mente va a disgusto, y por ello parca y malignamente sugiere sentencias y palabras" (I was in some ways coerced and did not so much follow my opinion as that of those who love me well . . . I do not deny that what happened to me, must happen to those who write out of necessity rather than out of a desire to do so, and as such do not agree with much of what they write. I am unhappy with myself about many things. The mind goes grudgingly when it is thus obliged and called to another place than to one it desires and as a result it suggests sentences and words in a brief and detrimental fashion). León, *Cantar de los cantares*, 13. The spirit in which Fray Luis writes these words is noticeably different from that of his original translation and commentary of the *Cantar* written *before* his trial.

74. León, *Cantar de cantares de Salomón*, 44.

75. Ibid., 47.

76. Ibid., 47–48.

77. Ibid., 59.

78. León, *A Bilingual Edition of Fray Luis De León's La Perfecta Casada*, 80–81.

79. Elliott, *Imperial Spain 1469–1716*, 285–320.

80. León, *A Bilingual Edition of Fray Luis De León's La Perfecta Casada*, 114–15.

81. Ibid., 26–27, emphasis added.
82. Ibid., 6–7.
83. Rivers, "El mar en la poesía de Fray Luis de León," 316.
84. León, *A Bilingual Edition of Fray Luis De León's La Perfecta Casada,* 86–87.
85. León, *Cantar de cantares de Salomón,* 12–13.

~

CHAPTER TWO

The ABCs of Marriage in Lope de Vega's *Peribáñez y el Comendador de Ocaña*

"No quiso la lengua castellana que de casado a cansado huviesse más de una letra de diferencia."

—Lope de Vega, *La Dorotea*

Lope de Vega's drama, *Peribáñez y el Comendador de Ocaña* begins with a wedding, the most significant rites of marriage. Since it is a "boda de villanos," that is, a peasant wedding, the festivities take place in a rural landscape, a space that Lope portrays with its attendant sense of informal and unrestrained joy. Music and dance add to the festive mood and even the priest plays the role of the fool or *gracioso*.[1] In the opening line of the play Inés, one of the revelers, wishes the newlyweds many years of joy ("Largos años os gocéis"), but the priest intervenes to admonish her:

Aunque no parecen mal,
son excusadas razones
para cumplimiento igual,
ni puede haber bendiciones
que igualen con el misal.
Hartas os dije; no queda
cosa que deciros pueda
el más deudo, el más amigo.[2]

[My children, though these courtesies sound well,
They're much too courtly, and superfluous.

No blessings equal those the prayer book gives.
I've wished you plenty; there's not one wish left
For even your dearest cousin or best friend
To give, not one.][3]

Here, the prayer book constitutes the last word on marriage; any additional blessings—or expressions of hymeneal pleasure—contradict the decorum of this religious ritual. In the context of a country wedding, the priest's observations may themselves appear excessive, and even "pedantic."[4] Moreover, he does not, in fact, have the last word on the subject, for the bride and groom continue to celebrate their love in verses that critics have long praised for their gorgeous pastoral imagery.[5] Although the priest again interrupts the bride and groom's dialogue, he does so to make way for a group of musicians, thus relinquishing any lingering reservations he might hold of nuptial celebrations.[6] The groom, Peribáñez, briefly raises the subject of jealousy and in doing so, foreshadows the play's predominant themes of adultery and dishonor; however, these are but passing shadows in the broader context of his betrothal to Casilda, the village's local beauty.[7] In short, the pervading tone of *Peribáñez*'s opening scene is that of a Bruegel-esque celebration where most members of the community join in the dance.

By opening the drama with a wedding scene, Lope establishes the preeminence of the conjugal bond in *Peribáñez*. Of the various practices associated with marriage in early modern Spain including courtship and widowhood, weddings are arguably its most public. Like the practices Georges Duby describes in his study of Medieval France, weddings in early modern Spain involve "publishing . . . and thereby socializing and legalizing a private act."[8] The wedding scene in *Peribáñez* is no exception, and in fact, goes a step further by taking the couple's union seriously. For all its merriment, the representation of marriage in *Peribáñez* marks a departure from previous literary models, for it represents the conjugal couple not as the object of comedy, but of serious drama or "tragicomedia" to borrow Lope's own term.[9] Ines's wish that the couple take *pleasure* in each other for many years to come—made explicit by the verb *gozar*—as well as her disingenuous retort to the priest's admonishments, endows the conjugal bond with an eroticism usually reserved for expressions of courtly love, mostly adulterous in nature. Not that this language is absent from the drama; later, the Comendador will give voice to his adulterous desire of the bride, thus threatening the couple's connubial bliss. However, *Peribáñez* reserves its most noteworthy expressions of mutual desire for the bride and groom and in doing so, elevates their status as characters worthy of attention.

Peribáñez not only exalts the institution of marriage but also contributes to disseminating its attendant values to a broad audience by dramatizing the themes of marital fidelity and honor for the stage. This is not to say that *Peribáñez* represents one-dimensional characters lacking in moral depth. Both Peribáñez and Casilda betray a peculiar attraction to material wealth and Peribáñez's recourse to violence far exceeds the standard defense of honor, factors that are crucial the moment Peribáñez decides to kill the Comendador, his lord and benefactor. This murder takes place after Peribáñez discovers the Comendador's repeated attempts to seduce his wife, Casilda. Peter Evans addresses the problematic nature of Peribáñez's killing of not only the Comendador, but also his accomplices "after an interval long enough to make him recognize the gravity of his action."[10] Evans adds that "Lope intends his audience to appreciate the extent of the savagery in the self Peribáñez has momentarily become."[11] Dian Fox takes this argument a step further by claiming that Peribáñez constitutes the true villain of the play; she argues that his actions are at least as, if not more, reprehensible than those of his adversary by acting not in the service "of a higher spiritual good, but of a most diabolical evil."[12] My own reading suggests that these characters are rendered more complex—and ultimately more compelling—if they are not held to absolute moral standards. If *Peribáñez* continues to be relevant to modern-day spectators and readers it is because its characters embody a combination of positive and negative attributes that can neither be reconciled nor fully satisfy expectations of poetic justice.

When Peribáñez kills not only the Comendador, but also Luján and Inés, it is not difficult to view in him "a savage, serial killer of three."[13] Although Luján and Inés are accomplices to the Comendador's attempted rape of Casilda, they are not the primary culprits. Casilda shares the more problematic dimensions of Peribáñez's murders given that she tacitly approves them; she "does not shrink at the shedding of blood" when Peribáñez kills Inés, who also happens to be her cousin.[14] Casilda further sanctions his murders by claiming in laconic terms that honor justifies the ultimate sacrifice: "No hay sangre donde hay honor" [There's no blood / Where honor lies].[15] Thus, even the most exemplary characters in *Peribáñez* possess moral flaws that render them more complex than the "perfect" husbands and wives of the didactic literature of the period. Still, it is worth recalling that Casilda is on the verge of being raped when Peribáñez commits the murders and that the couple's social class prevents them from defending themselves, regardless of the outrage committed against them. How *Peribáñez* adheres to the morality prescribed by the didactic literature while creating a compelling drama for public consumption is arguably one of its most remarkable achievements. One way of understanding how Lope produces this tension between didacticism and drama, that is, his "doble faceta de propaganda y subversion" (double facet of propaganda and subversion), is by considering how *Peribáñez* engages these respective discourses over the course of the action.[16]

Peribáñez invokes the more conventional definition of the conjugal bond when he declares to Casilda that she is his wife according to both divine and human laws.[17] That the Comendador later pays lip service to this same definition of marriage in his perfunctory response to Peribáñez suggests its conventional nature: "Tenéis razón de amar a quien os ama, / por ley divina y por humanas leyes" (You're right, by law of heaven and earthly laws, / To love the wife that loves you in return).[18] Here the Comendador contradicts his adulterous intentions and reveals the degree to which he is conscious of his trespasses against the laws governing marriage. More importantly, the Comendador suggests that reason—as opposed to passion—governs Peribáñez's love for Casilda ("Tenéis *razón*") insinuating that an underwhelming sense of duty binds them in matrimony rather than the overwhelming sense of desire that defines his own attraction to her. These exchanges suggest that secular and religious laws rather than love or even mutual attraction are the primary basis of marriage. While there is much to suggest such a view throughout the play, the lengths to which Peribáñez goes to protect his marriage, indicate otherwise.

In no other scene is the inherent didacticism in relation to marriage more apparent than when Peribáñez and Casilda initiate their honeymoon by listing, in alphabetical order, their respective duties as husband and wife:

CASILDA.   ¿Qué ha de tener para buena una mujer?

PERIBÁÑEZ.   Oye.

CASILDA.   Di.

PERIBÁÑEZ.   Amar y honrar su marido
es letra deste abecé,
siendo buena por la B,
que es todo el bien que te pido.
Haráte cuerda la C,
la D dulce y entendida
la E, y la F en la vida
firme, fuerte, y de gran fe.[19]

[CASILDA.   What must a woman have
To make a good wife?

PERIBÁÑEZ.   Listen.

CASILDA.   Tell me, love.

PERIBÁÑEZ.   Adore her husband always is the A
That starts this ABC; and for the B
Be beautiful and bonny, since that's best.
The C will make you careful, D discreet,
E ever-wise, equal to every task,
F firm and fair and faithful to the end.][20]

The alphabetical order in which Peribáñez recites his wife's duties under-scores the presumably fundamental nature of her responsibilities to love, honor, and obey him. While the primary purpose of Peribáñez's alphabetical list is to provide Casilda with a mnemonic device for carrying out her wifely duties, these ABCs also evoke a kind of basic knowledge akin to reading and writing. In other words, Peribáñez posits the conjugal life as a kind of language that must be memorized in order to be successful. He exhorts Casilda to learn this language in order for them to achieve wedded bliss and even refers to it in academic terms: "Aprende este canto llano; / que, con aqueste cartilla, / tú serás flor de la villa, / y yo el más noble villano" (Learn this plain chant, Casilda, / And it will make you all Ocaña's flower, / and me the noblest of its villagers).[21] By this definition, marriage possesses a textbook-like quality, its own simple narrative or "canto llano" where spontaneous expressions of affection are all but absent. That a code is even needed suggests that marriage's virtues are not innate or natural but rather acquired through learning.

What, exactly, is the nature of a wife's duties according to Peribáñez? He summarizes them the moment he and Casilda cross the proverbial threshold for the first time as newlyweds:

Ya estamos en nuestra casa,
Su dueño y mío has de ser;
Ya sabes que la mujer
Para obedecer se casa . . .[22]

[Casilda, now we're in our house, alone,
You have to be its master and mine too.
You know a wife gets married to obey.][23]

Peribáñez's twice-repeated "casa" in this passage refers both to "house" and the act of "marrying." The pun epitomizes Casilda's duties: to marry means to come home, to possess and be possessed by a domestic space. The next chapter explores in more detail the intricate etymological relation between these words, but suffice it to say that in *Peribáñez* the relationship between casa-casado is very close. While Casilda is "lord" of her home ("dueño"), she is also lorded over by Peribáñez who makes plain that she must obey him ("ya sabes que la mujer / para obedecer se casa").[24] Her actions over the course of the drama confirm this aspect of her identity in that conflict ensues every time the Comendador attempts to violate this space while she protects it from him.

Casilda proves to be just as authoritative as her husband as she proceeds to recite his duties, again in alphabetical order. To his credit, Peribáñez does not resist this new, subordinate role: "Yo me ofrezco, prenda mía, / a saber este abecé" (I volunteer to learn this alphabet).[25] Her recitation suggests her competency in mastering the "language" of the conjugal life and that she is prepared to play the role of teacher as well as that of student. Although Peribáñez's alphabet is somewhat more complete—Casilda skips over "E" and "Z"—she may exceed him where wordplay is concerned. While Peribáñez assigns the letter "X" to the word *"cristiana"* ("X" corresponding to the Greek "Christ"), Casilda employs this letter as a pretext to embrace Peribáñez:

> por la X con abiertos
> braços imitarla ansí,
>
> (*abrázale*)
>
> y como estamos aquí
> estemos después de muertos.[26]
>
> [And as for X, let's imitate it now
>
> (*She hugs him*)
>
> With arms that open tenderly, and love,
> As we are now, let's stay so, even in death.][27]

On the one hand, this final physical flourish on Casilda's part represents an open—and for seventeenth-century Spanish letters, unusual—display of spousal affection.[28] On the other hand, her words express the view espoused by moralists of the period that marriage represents a bond capable of transcending death. Regardless of whether Casilda outdoes her husband in the alphabet game, their respective recitals compliment rather than contradict each other. Both Casilda and Peribáñez emphasize the importance of honor and fidelity in their respective alphabets, qualities that will later become central to Casilda's steadfast resistance to the Comendador's adulterous advances.

This reciprocity between husband and wife assumes that they conduct themselves according to preassigned gender roles. For example, Peribáñez calls on Casilda to be the teacher of their progeny—"Maestra de tus hijos"— while no mention is made of his role in the rearing of children.[29] Rather, she exhorts him to be a gentleman ("galán") as well as a father to her ("Por la P me has de hazer obras de padre").[30] These small but significant differences indicate the manner in which *Peribáñez* constructs spousal roles along gender lines with tremendous significance for the outcome of the play. For instance, the importance of gender is apparent early in the drama when Casilda restrains Peribáñez from joining in the collective effort to rein in a bull that bursts upon the scene of their wedding:

> No conviene a tu decoro
> el día que te has casado,
> ni que un rezién deposado
> se ponga en cuernos de un toro.[31]

> [It isn't proper on your wedding day.
> The bridegroom shouldn't tangle with the horns
> Of bulls, my love—(*slyly*) or with any other horns.][32]

While Peribáñez refrains from such emblematic demonstrations of macho bravado as bullfighting, the Comendador directly engages in the fight—the latter is, after all, a bachelor. According to Casilda, decorum prevents a recently married man from placing himself within range of the bull's horns, and while Peribáñez concedes, he does so on different grounds, claiming that even the mere mention of horns—read *cornudo* or cuckold—fills him with dread.[33] The stigma attached to cuckoldry represents a literary commonplace of early modern Spanish letters, and this exchange between the newlyweds is no exception. It is a stigma from which Peribáñez will actively seek to protect himself as the Comendador's adulterous advances toward Casilda become more aggressive. Peribáñez's fear of cuckoldry responds in large measure to his society's expectations of what it means to be a man; to meet these demands implies success, to fall short of them, utter failure.

The pedagogical qualities of Peribáñez and Casilda's ABCs invite a return to the didactic literature on marriage of the previous chapter. In more ways than one, their alphabetical recital summarizes the lessons contained in works such as Juan Luis Vives's *Educación de la mujer cristiana* and Fray Luis de León's *La perfecta casada*. But the active role Casilda plays in responding to her husband's instruction as she takes on the role of his teacher points to guides that were not only directed to a female audience but also a male one. While guides for wives appeared with increasing frequency in sixteenth-century Spain, those for husbands were rare and have received comparatively less critical attention.[34] Juan Luis Vives's *Deberes del marido* (*A Husband's Duties*) published in 1528 is exceptional in this regard.

In Vives's dedicatory remarks to *Deberes del marido*, he recognizes its exceptional nature when admitting that it had never crossed his mind to write such a guide until readers of his previous guide for women, *Educación de la mujer crisitiana* demanded a parallel guide for men (1259).[35] Although Vives dedicates this work to a male readership, *Deberes del marido* is "a book which, in a revealing manner, has much more to say about the obligations of wives than those of husbands."[36] For the most part, *Deberes del marido* represents morality in conventional terms in its numerous references to classical and biblical sources regarding women as the "weaker" sex. Still, its occasional references to specifically female experiences such as pregnancy and menstruation suggest a kind of sexual education that distinguishes it from previous works on women's education. While these are not subjects that appear in *Peribáñez*, they do suggest the degree to which *Deberes del marido* distinguishes itself from its predecessors; like *Peribáñez*, it also suggests an increasing awareness of the singular role women play within this society.

Where *Deberes del marido* bears a relation to *Peribáñez* is in the connection it draws between marriage and domesticity by assigning a wife's place within the home:

> La casa sea para ella tan ancha y holgada como la mayor de las ciudades, de modo que salga raras veces y que le parezca que va a emprender una peregrinación a Tierra Santa, Roma o Santiago todas las veces que tuviese que sacar el pie afuera.[37]

> [May the house be as large and as comfortable as the greatest of cities so that she will rarely go out, and every time she sets foot outside her home, it will seem as though she is embarking on a pilgrimage to the Holy Land, Rome, or Santiago.]

Here the narrator exhorts a husband to provide his wife with accommodations so spacious that she rarely, if ever, ventures beyond its walls. In the context of *Peribáñez*, this recommendation takes on particular relevance, for it is precisely the couple's pilgrimage to Toledo to celebrate the festivities marking the Feast of the Assumption of the Virgin that provides the Comendador with the opportunity he seeks to intensify his pursuit of Casilda. Although the distance separating Ocaña from Toledo is nowhere as significant as that of the Holy Land, Rome, or even Santiago de Compostela, the peasants' elaborate preparations for the trip underscore the importance it takes on for them. Casilda and her companions refer to their clothing for the trip in loving detail, while Peribáñez requests a tapestry from the Comendador to embellish his horse-drawn cart, a request that will have far-reaching consequences for all involved as we will later see.[38]

However, *Peribáñez* does not suggest a cautionary tale against women venturing beyond the walls of their homes. While *Deberes del marido* makes its condemnation of wandering women explicit, there is little evidence in *Peribáñez* to suggest such a moral; after all, the religious purpose of the trip provides ample justification for the women's departure from hearth and home. What *Peribáñez* posits as morally problematic is both the female and male characters' focus on material wealth in preparation for the trip, a preoccupation that becomes apparent the moment Peribáñez and his entourage leave for Toledo. In this respect, both *Peribáñez* and *Deberes del marido* share a deep concern for domestic economy that translates as a warning against living beyond one's means. For example, when Casilda and her female companions prepare for their trip to Toledo, their attire is more elaborate than what one might expect of a peasant. One of the women wears a dress embroidered in silver, "Yo llevo unos cuerpos llenos / de pasamanos de plata" (Mine is embroidered with fine silver threads) while Casilda is decked in a red velvet skirt befitting her newly acquired status as a married woman: "son / galas de mujer casada" (every married woman wears for best).[39] The women's physical appearance not only offers a vivid theatrical spectacle, but also suggests the manner in which their interest in material goods outweighs any spiritual concerns motivating their religious pilgrimage.

In a Spanish version of keeping up with the Joneses, Peribáñez expresses disappointment when he sees his neighbor's richly adorned cart in preparation for the trip: "Pena, Casilda, me ha dado / El ver que el carro de Bras / lleva alhombra y repostero" (I felt annoyed, Casilda, when I saw / Blas in his cart with carpets on the seats and an embroidered mantle on the horse).[40] Peribáñez does not need such superficial trappings, for all signs point to the material comforts and prestige he enjoys within his community, his peasant status notwithstanding. Nonetheless, Peribáñez goes out of his way to acquire a rich tapestry from the Comendador who is all too eager to place his vassal in his debt. The Comendador has already made explicit his plans to follow the advice of his lackey to bribe Peribáñez by offering him two mules, while bestowing a pair of gold hoop earrings on Casilda.[41] It is significant that the silk tapestry the Comendador finally gives to Peribáñez carries the aristocrat's coat of arms for it later serves to adorn Casilda's bedroom suggesting the Comendador's symbolic presence in the couple's most intimate domestic space. It is therefore not surprising that when Peribáñez first perceives the Comendador's advances toward Casilda, he orders her to take down the tapestry, a command with which she promptly complies.

Deberes del marido underscores the virtues of frugality and hard work. A husband who lives at his wife's expense incurs the narrator's strongest condemnation: "cuán miserables y abyectos son aquellos maridos que quitan a sus esposas unos dineros que se juegan a los naipes o se tragan en glotonerías. . . . Los hombres que tal hacen, por su malicia, por su degenerada pequeñez de alma, son inferiores a las bestias" (how miserable and abject are those husbands who take away money from their wives to play cards or to stuff themselves with delicacies. . . . Men who do such things are, because of their malice and their degenerate, small souls, inferior to beasts).[42] Peribáñez represents an exemplary provider rather than the "miserable and abject" gambler-husband Vives describes here. Nonetheless, in both the dramatic and didactic discourses, economic and conjugal matters are inseparable. When Peribáñez and Casilda are married, the couple expresses their love in the first scene by transforming the ordinary, everyday objects of farm life into ones of extraordinary beauty. Peribáñez initiates the exchange and draws on a broad range of images from the Spanish countryside. In this verbal *pas-a-deux* between the couple, Peribáñez names mainly raw materials—olives, apples, wine, grapes, and wheat—while Casilda extends the list by adding manufactured products such as shoes, shirts, candles, and bread. Together, the couple creates an image of agricultural plenitude.

Casilda takes quite a different view of material goods when the Comendador, disguised as a farmer, attempts to gain entry into her home in order to seduce her. Her rejection of him suggests that she is well aware of his disguise as she proceeds to describe in detail the kind of woman he would, in fact, be likely to court:

El Comendador de Ocaña
servirá dama de estima,

no con sayuelo de grana
ni con saya de palmilla.
Copete traerá rizado
gorguera de holanda fina,
no cofia de pinos tosca,
y toca de argentería.
En coche o silla de seda
los disantos irá a missa;
no vendrá en carro de estacas
de los campos a las viñas.
Dírale en cartas discretas
requiebros a maravilla,
no labradores desdenes,
envueltos en señorías.
Olerále a guantes de ámbar,
a perfumes y pastillas;
no a tomillo ni cantueso,
poleo y zarzas floridas.[43]

[The Commander of Ocaña
Woos a lady fair and fine,
Not for her a shawl of scarlet,
Nor a skirt of deep blue dye.
She will curl her hair in ringlets
With a ruff of lace beside,
She'll not wear a simple bonnet
With a net of silver twine.
She will go to church on Sundays
In a coach with gilded side,
She'll not travel in a hay cart
From the farmyard to the vines.
She will tell him clever nothings
In the letters that she writes,
Not sharp words of village anger
Wrapped in "If you'll be so kind."
She will smell of gloves in amber,
Perfumes, musk and precious spice,
Not of brambles and wild roses,
Mint and lavender and thyme.][44]

Here, artifice epitomizes the appearance of an aristocratic woman: her curled forelock, fine Dutch collar, and amber perfumed gloves point to

Baroque objects of feminine refinement. In contrast, the peasant woman wears objects borrowed almost exclusively from the natural world: her hair is adorned with rough pine, and the earth endows her with the natural fragrance of thyme, lavender, and mint. Casilda adds that aristocrats and peasants do not even share the same language of courtship; the aristocrat pays his compliments to his lady indirectly by means of billet-doux, whereas the peasant directly rebuffs such expressions with "rustic disdain" ("labradores desdenes"). Casilda's reply to the Comendador is careful not to criticize the women whose social class he shares. But in case it is not clear where her sympathies lie, she famously adds her preference for Peribáñez in his rough cape to the Comendador who dons a richly embroidered one: "más quiero yo a Peribáñez / con su capa la pardilla / que al Comendador de Ocaña con la suya guarnecida" (I love more my Peribáñez / In his cloack of simple style, / Than Ocaña's bold Commander / In his own that's gold and shines).[45]

Casilda's superb rhetorical skills in her speech to the Comendador reveal substantial knowledge of the linguistic artifice she attributes to others beside herself. The distinction she draws between the art with which the aristocrat adorns herself and the peasant's natural world disregards the basis of its own construction. The space separating aristocratic and peasant women—or Casilda and the Comendador, for that matter—does not, in fact, spring from nature, but rather is deeply embedded in the social order. In Casilda's speech, numerous references to clothing embody the tensions between the classes. As we have seen, Casilda prefers her husband in his humble hunting attire to the Comendador decked in diamond studded sleeves and a silk cap. Casilda's speech culminates in the comparison she draws between the roughly hewn stone cross of her village to the red cross of the military order of Santiago embroidered on the Comendador's doublet: "más devoción me causa / la cruz de piedra en la ermita, / que la roja de Santiago / en su bordada ropilla" (As I reverence more the stone cross / Standing in Saint Roch's shrine / Than the red one of Santiago / On his lordship's shirt inscribed).[46] The lasting nature of the stone cross stands in stark contrast to the ephemeral quality of the cross of Santiago, one of early modern Spain's most important status symbols.[47] Casilda's final rebuff comes as a surprise given that until this moment, her terms of comparison were between the Comendador and her husband. Here, however, she suggests that the real source of her devotion is neither the worldly pleasures of a husband or lover, much less the material objects that clothe them. Rather, Casilda suggests that she is devoted to a higher, more enduring spiritual order symbolized by the stone cross.

Another irony of the distinction Casilda draws between social and economic classes is that it places her at a distinct disadvantage to her aristocratic counterparts. In her rejection of the Comendador's adulterous advances, she employs an argument that reminds him of the privileges he enjoys by virtue of the superior social position he occupies. It is a curious argument, for it preserves a social order that has little to offer her. However, there is an underlying recognition on the part of Casilda that the Comendador has little to lose by courting her, whereas she risks not only her reputation but even her life. That this is, in fact, the case is born out by her cousin Inés who is courted by one of the Comendador's lackeys, Leonardo. He has ulterior motives, specifically to win Inés's confidence so that the Comendador may gain easy entry into Casilda and Peribáñez's home. When these motives are brought to light, Peribáñez murders both Leonardo and Inés and Casilda fully sanctions these deaths in the name of honor.

The drama's pastoral vision takes a decidedly different turn the moment it becomes clear to Peribáñez that the Comendador threatens to destroy their marriage. Peribáñez reduces the broad expanse of land and its bounty to a single reed he compares to the concept of honor. He characterizes honor as a reed that is hollow, fragile, and even "vil" (vile):

> Caña de honor quebradiça,
> caña hueca y sin sustancia,
> de hojas de poca importancia,
> con que su tronco entapiza.
> ¡Oh caña, toda aparato,
> caña fantástica y vil,
> para quebrada sutil,
> y verde tan breve rato!
> [. . .] Aquí naciste en Ocaña
> conmigo al viento ligero;
> yo te cortaré primero
> que te quiebres, débil caña.[48]

> [O fragile cane of honour, hollow wand,
> Vain, insubstantial straw, what sorry leaves
> Wrap round the wretched pipe of its mean trunk!
> Ocaña, honour's cane, all outward tricks
> Fantastic, paltry stem, so light to break
> And green indeed, indeed, so short a time!
> [. . .] Here in Ocaña you were born with me,
> In this light wind; and here I'll cut you down
> Frail cane, before you're broken.][49]

Peribáñez's metaphor extends beyond that of honor to encompass his village by means of the play on words, *caña* ("reed") and *Ocaña*. The seamless connection between the landscape and honor in effect naturalizes a socially constructed concept that, in the context of the drama, is bound up in Peribáñez's reputation as a married man. Alone, he cannot protect this reputation, for his honor does not depend exclusively on him, but on others' willingness to uphold—or in the case of the Comendador—degrade it. Despite the critical tone of this soliloquy, it is not altogether clear whether Peribáñez resists or conforms to his society's concept of honor. In claiming that he will "cut down" this fragile stalk before it breaks on its own, he may be foreshadowing his murder of the Comendador, or more ominously, that of his own wife.

What is clear is that the Comendador's trespasses trigger an internal struggle in Peribáñez. His soliloquy signals a shift from the metaphorical characterization of the landscape to the literal "cutting down" or murder of the Comendador. This struggle centers on Peribáñez's place in the feudal order that demands he submit to the higher authority of the Comendador no matter how arbitrarily the Comendador may exercise it. On the one hand, Peribáñez must "honor" the social hierarchy and his place in it, what Correa refers to as a "vertical" sense of honor.[50] On the other hand, personal honor demands swift vengeance for any infidelities committed against or by his wife, in short anything that might lead him to wear the dreaded horns of the cuckold. Thus, Peribáñez's public, as well as his private sense of honor, stands in direct contradiction until the dénouement in which he restores both.

In the third and final act of the drama, Peribáñez entrusts his home and wife to the care of the Comendador, although he is fully aware of the threat the aristocrat poses to both of them.[51] Initially, Peribáñez's motives for placing Casilda in danger are not altogether clear; however, as the action unfolds, it becomes apparent that this represents a calculated risk on his part. At the most basic level, abandoning his wife allows him to confirm his suspicions of the Comendador's adulterous intentions, while simultaneously allowing him to dispel any doubts he might hold regarding Casilda's fidelity. Just as importantly, it permits Peribáñez to avenge his honor without suffering the fatal consequences that the killing of an aristocrat by a peasant necessarily entails. By requesting that the Comendador knight him before Peribáñez leaves to fight on his behalf, Peribáñez secures the right to defend his honor at all costs—a request the Comendador all too gladly accepts in order to expedite Peribáñez's departure. In the end, Peribáñez's strategy succeeds as the monarchs who appear at the conclusion pardon his murder.

Notwithstanding the enormous social and economic differences separating the monarchs from the peasants, their appearance in *Peribáñez* offers an alternative and powerful image of a conjugal couple. Dian Fox notes how earlier in the dramatic action, Peribáñez refers to himself and his wife as king and queen, thus reinforcing the parallel between the respective couples and adds that Lope depicts Enrique III and Katherine of Lancaster as a "loving couple."[52] Indeed, the King's terms of endearment when deferring to the Queen in critical matters of state—in this case, the war against the infidel— suggests just such an image:

> ¿Qué puedo yo tratar de paz, señora,
> En que vos no podáis darme consejo?
> Y es de guerra lo que trato agora,
> ¿cuándo con vos, mi bien, no me aconsejo?[53]

> [When do I talk of peace and not invite
> Your sound advice, given with such thoughtful care
> And if, as now, it's war that we must fight,
> When don't I ask for your good counsel there?][54]

Rather than represent the royal couple as exclusively bound by political prerogatives, their exchanges at the conclusion of the drama indicate they are also united by mutual affection. The monarchs thus epitomize the harmony that marriage can bring to the personal as well as political sphere. By deferring to his wife's authority, the king spares Peribáñez's life thus ensuring a felicitous end to the drama. The juxtaposition of bellicose and sentimental expressions in the monarchs' exchange may strike the contemporary reader/ spectator as being strangely at odds with each other. In similar fashion, the representation of the monarchs as a doting couple would have struck Lope's audience as highly unconventional, particularly in an age when such liaisons were based first and foremost on political rather than personal prerogatives.[55]

In the epigraph cited at the beginning of this chapter, "No quiso la lengua castellana que de casado a cansado huviesse más de una letra de diferencia" (The Spanish language did not want more than a single letter to distinguish [the words] marriage from exhaustion), Lope casts a satiric eye on the institution of marriage by observing the proximity between the words *casado* ("married") and *cansado* ("tired," "exhausted"). Lope's observation points not only to the difference a single letter can make, but also to a commonplace whereby marriage constitutes a burden, weighing heavily on the couple as a kind of proverbial yoke. However, the semantic shift between *cansado* and *casado* contains implications that extend far beyond Lope's word play and indirectly take us back to Peribáñez and Casilda's original alphabet. Henri Mérimée notes how various editions of *Peribáñez* are inconsistent in the scene where Peribáñez prepares a battalion of farmers alongside the Comendador's own group of aristocrats. In the 1614 edition, Casilda and her neighbors observe the military preparations, whereupon one of the women makes patent where her sympathies lie:

INÉS.   ¿Qué es esto?

COSTANÇA.   La compañía
de los hidalgos *cansados*.

INÉS.   Más luzidos han salido
nuestros fuertes labradores.

COSTANÇA.   Si son las galas mejores,
Los ánimos no lo han sido.[56]

[INÉS.   What's this?

COSTANÇA.   The company of gentlemen.
How drab they look.

INÉS.   The clothes they wear may shine,
And yet their spirits are as dull as lead.][57]

Mérimée brings attention to the incongruity between the 1614 edition and that of 1857; the first describes the aristocrats as "tired" (*cansado*) whereas in the second, more illogical version they are "married" (*casados*). Other critics since Mérimée extend his initial finding by revealing the underlying anti-Semitic critique of the aristocracy in the women's exchange: "*cansado* se refiere aquí a la ley del Antiguo Testamento, con lo cual se hace más punzante el dicterio de los labriegos. . . . Es decir, que *cansado* tomó sentido tan antijudaico como *esperar*" (here *cansado* [tired, weary] refers to the laws of the Old Testament, thus rendering the peasants' comments all the more biting. . . . That is to say, *cansado* took on the anti-Jewish meaning of *waiting*).[58] Not only are the women's anti-Semitic remarks significant in their implicit criticism of the aristocracy, but such views also play a decisive role in Peribáñez and Casilda's marriage in ways that are perhaps not obvious at first sight.

In the couple's recital of the ABCs of marriage, Peribáñez exhorts Casilda to be clean ("Limpia serás por la L"). His demand might appear to involve household matters were it not for the various references to cleanliness in the specific context of blood purity that frames the drama. In a decisive moment of Peribáñez's defense of the Comendador's murder, he argues to the King and Queen of Spain that his background is untainted by Jewish or Muslim blood:

Yo soy un hombre
aunque de villana casta,
limpio de sangre, y jamás
de hebrea o mora manchada.
Fui el mejor de mis iguales,
Y, en cuantas cosas trataban,
Me dieron primero voto,
Y truxe seis años vara.
Caséme con la que ves,
también *limpia* aunque villana;
virtuosa; si la ha visto
la envidia assida a la fama.[59]

[I am a man who, though of peasant's rank,
Has blood that's pure, not stained with Moors' or Jews'.
Mine was the leading voice among my peers,
Whatever they discussed I had first vote,
And six years long I held the staff, as mayor.
I married her you see, her blood's pure too,
Though she's a peasant, virtuous as the day,
And carping envy never faulted her.][60]

Here blood purity constitutes a key element of Peribáñez's defense in the murder of an aristocrat. The absence of Jewish or Muslim blood presumably trumps his status as a peasant—his recent knighthood notwithstanding—the implication being that its possible presence in the Comendador detracts from his noble status. Moreover, Peribáñez's marriage to Casilda, whom he also defines as "clean" in this passage, guarantees future generations of "clean" Christians. The King accepts this defense and even rewards Peribáñez by, among other things, granting him a title and the right to bear arms while the Queen gives four of her dresses to Casilda. One of the greatest ironies of the drama is that the material honors the monarchs bestow on the couple are the very ones Peribáñez and Casilda had previously rejected in order to safeguard their marriage. By the conclusion of the drama, Peribáñez resembles the Comendador more than ever in his newly acquired status as captain, in the arms he bears, and even in his speech.

Peribáñez and Casilda's marriage thus withstands the pressures wrought by the Comendador through a combination of strategies, from Casilda's resistance to Peribáñez's appeal to the monarchs' authority. *Peribáñez* stands apart from other dramas of the period where even innocent wives are not spared the violence of rape or murder.[61] And yet, the success of Casilda and Peribáñez's marriage is predicated on another kind of violence. Racial and religious bigotry—translated as the obsession with blood purity—traverses the drama, including the seemingly childlike guise of the ABCs of marriage. The couple's adherence to these lessons suggests that they emerge unscathed from the conflict precisely because they uphold its dictates at all costs, and in the end, are rewarded for it. If Peribáñez receives the King's pardon, it is not because the injustice of the feudal system has been revealed to the King who, to the very end, remains struck by the great stock a peasant places in his honor: "¡Cosa extraña! / ¡Qué un labrador tan humilde / estime tanto su fama!" (Strange event! That this poor man, / A peasant, should so cherish his good name!).[62] Rather, the King sees in Peribáñez a man of great worth ("un hombre deste valor") based on the dictates of blood purity, the "justice" of which were subject to serious question in early modern Spain. In the end, Peribáñez as well as Casilda become part of the very order that makes such injustices possible.

Notes

1. According to John T. Boorman, "[t]he very presence of the Priest—not a common figure in the *comedia*—draws attention to the fact that the single act uniting Peribáñez and Casilda is both a valid contract in the eyes of the law and an indissoluble sacrament in the eyes of Heaven." Boorman, "Divina Ley and Derecho Humano," in *Peribáñez*, 12. The contractual nature of the conjugal bond plays a significant role in *Peribáñez*, since it will come into serious question the moment the Comendador attempts to seduce the wife of one of his vassals.

2. Vega, *Peribáñez y el Comendador de Ocaña*, lines 6–13.

3. Vega, *Peribáñez and the Comendador*, lines 8–13.

4. Wilson, "Image et structure dans 'Peribáñez,'" 128.

5. In reference to Peribáñez and Casilda's exchange in this opening scene, E. M. Wilson observes: "Both speeches are charming. Each naïf and familiar image is rendered vivid by specific details. It is the very poetry of daily life." Wilson, "Image et structure dans 'Peribáñez,'" 130. Gustavo Correa refers to the same scene as "the epitome of a world of plenty as it is lived and experienced cyclically in the rural life." Correa, "El doble aspecto de la honra en *Peribáñez y el comendador de Ocaña*," 191.

6. The musician's song brings harmony to the dispute between the priest and Inés by assigning God and the fields—rather than the priest or the revelers—the task of bringing good tidings to the couple: "Y a los nuevos desposados / eche Dios su bendición; / parabién les den los prados, / pues hoy para en uno son" (God bless

the bride, God bless the groom, / with many years of life. / The fields shall sing this glad morning that made them man and wife). Vega, *Peribáñez y el Comendador de Ocaña*, lines 142–45. Vega, *Peribáñez and the Comendador*, lines 162–65. Stephanie Coontz observes that "Protestants and Catholics alike began to condemn the noisy public rituals that had marked a community's acceptance or rejection of marriage. We have already seen what a fracas could break out when a community in the late Middle Ages disapproved of a particular wedding. They escorted the newlyweds to bed, playing loud music and making sexual jokes." Coontz, *Marriage, a History*, 135.

7. Vega, *Peribáñez y el Comendador de Ocaña*, lines 19–20.

8. Duby, *Love and Marriage in the Middle Ages*, 11.

9. Noël Salomón refers to Peribáñez as "un villano digno" (a dignified peasant) and comments extensively on the transformation of this character over the course of the Spanish drama. According to Salomón, Peribáñez is neither comic nor tragic, but rather a hybrid figure who distinguishes himself by claiming dignity for a broader peasant class: "In reality, it is the right to dignity shared by all the peasants of Castile that Peribáñez inscribes in blood in this tragedy. . . . Peribáñez summarizes the entire dramatic trajectory of the peasant, achieving tragedy through comedy." Salomon, *Lo villano en el teatro del Siglo de Oro*, 700.

10. Evans, "*Peribáñez* and Ways of Looking at Golden Age Dramatic Characters," 147.

11. Ibid.

12. Fox, *Refiguring the Hero*, 127.

13. Fischer, "Staging Lope de Vega's *Peribáñez*," 168.

14. See J. M. Ruano and J. E. Varey in Vega, *Peribáñez y el Comendador de Ocaña*, 26.

15. Vega, *Peribáñez y el Comendador de Ocaña*, line 810. Vega, *Peribáñez and the Comendador*, lines 2897–98.

16. Delgado-Morales, "Palabra y ornato en la puesta en escena de Peribáñez y Fuenteovejuna," 341. In J. M. Ruano and J. E. Varey's introductory remarks to their edition of *Peribáñez* they articulate the dramatic tension as follows: "*Peribáñez* is a play which sets out to reinforce the accepted social order, whilst demonstrating the way in which the actions of the individual can subvert the temporal system." Vega, *Peribáñez y el Comendador de Ocaña*, 54.

17. Vega, *Peribáñez y el Comendador de Ocaña*, lines 70–80.

18. Ibid., lines 883–85.

19. Ibid., lines 406–15.

20. Vega, *Peribáñez and the Comendador*, lines 405–13.

21. Vega, *Peribáñez y el Comendador de Ocaña*, lines 444–48. Juan María Marín remarks in his edition of *Peribáñez* that "*Canto llano*" refers to those notes or points proceed with equal and uniform sound and rhythmical measure. . . . Despite this definition, a more fitting sense seems that of a 'simple narration.'" Their differences notwithstanding, these definitions of *canto llano* underscore its pedagogical qualities.

22. Vega, *Peribáñez y el Comendador de Ocaña*, lines 396–99.

23. Vega, *Peribáñez and the Comendador*, lines 394–97.

24. Peter Evans sees in Casilda's name yet another reference to this domestic space or "casa." Evans, "*Peribáñez* and Ways of Looking at Golden Age Dramatic Characters," 139.

25. Vega, *Peribáñez y el Comendador de Ocaña*, lines 487–88. Vega, *Peribáñez and the Comendador*, line 488.

26. Vega, *Peribáñez y el Comendador de Ocaña*, lines 484–87.

27. Vega, *Peribáñez and the Comendador*, lines 483–85.

28. Boscán's lyric, "Repuesta de Boscán a Don Diego de Mendoza" is exceptional in its praise of the author's wife and more generally of the married life. For further discussion, see Introduction.

29. Vega, *Peribáñez y el Comendador de Ocaña*, lines 484–87.

30. Ibid., lines 465, 476–77.

31. Ibid., lines 214–17.

32. Vega, *Peribáñez and the Comendador*, lines 213–15.

33. Vega, *Peribáñez y el Comendador de Ocaña*, lines 218–21.

34. Olga Rivera focuses on the representation of women in *Deberes del marido* and concludes that "In the rhetoric regarding 'women's natural condition' formulated in *Deberes del marido*, the emphasis that Vives places on reinterpreting on so-called feminine pains and defects resulting from the 'feminine condition' should not be underestimated; he did not consider them to appear equally in all women nor were they exclusive of the female sex. On the other hand, Vives subscribes to and divulges the prevailing ideas of the period regarding female weakness." Rivera, *Deberes del marido*, lines 484–87.

35. Vives describes the genesis of his *Deberes del marido* as follows: "Cuando, años atrás, iba escribiendo el tratado acerca de la formación de la mujer cristiana, poco podía yo pensar que en lo sucesivo no habían de faltar quienes me exhortasen a escribir un tratadillo análogo acerca de los deberes del marido, y aun he de confesar que tal idea no me vino jamás a las mientes" (When, years ago, I was writing a treatise on the education of Christian women, I never thought that there would afterwards be those who exhorted me to write a little analogous treatise on a husband's duties, and I even have to have confess that such a thought never crossed my mind). Vives, *Obras completas*, 1259.

36. Noreña, "Juan Luis Vives on the Relations between the Sexes," 451.

37. Vives, *Obras completas*, 1329.

38. Vega, *Peribáñez y el Comendador de Ocaña*, lines 662–93. Manuel Delgado-Morales comments on the relationship between these possessions and the mise-en-scène: "the stage directions in *Peribáñez* tend to accentuate the importance of appearances in an individual brought about by a change of costume. In other words, in contrast to the relatively stark costuming of *Fuenteovejuna*, *Peribáñez* displays exuberant clothes and colors, where even the characteristics of the character's cos-

tumes are indicated." Delgado-Morales, "Palabra y ornato en la puesta en escena de *Peribáñez y Fuenteovejuna*," 356.

39. Vega, *Peribáñez y el Comendador de Ocaña*, lines 669–75. Vega, *Peribáñez and the Comendador*, lines 670, 672–74.

40. Vega, *Peribáñez y el Comendador de Ocaña*, lines 666–71.

41. Ibid., lines 594–600.

42. Vives, *Obras completas*, 1328.

43. Vega, *Peribáñez y el Comendador de Ocaña*, lines 521–40.

44. Vega, *Peribáñez and the Comendador*, lines 1570–89.

45. Vega, *Peribáñez y el Comendador de Ocaña*, lines 545–48; Vega, *Peribáñez and the Comendador*, lines 1594–97.

46. Vega, *Peribáñez y el Comendador de Ocaña*, lines 561–64.

47. Diego de Velázquez also wears one in his portrait of *Las Meninas*, and Lope himself obtained the coveted cross. For more on the Order of Santiago see Elliott, *Imperial Spain 1469–1716*, 88–89.

48. Vega, *Peribáñez y el Comendador de Ocaña*, lines 541–56.

49. Vega, *Peribáñez and the Comendador*, lines 2630–35.

50. Correa, "El doble aspecto de la honra en *Peribáñez y el comendador de Ocaña*."

51. Vega, *Peribáñez y el Comendador de Ocaña*, lines 181–84.

52. Fox, *Refiguring the Hero*, 119.

53. Vega, *Peribáñez y el Comendador de Ocaña*, 846–50.

54. Vega, *Peribáñez and the Comendador*, lines 2931–35. The translator does not translate the phrase "mi bien" from the original; it is a term of endearment much like "my dear" or "my love."

55. The action of *Peribáñez* takes place in the fourteenth century, although there are relatively few references to the past in this work. The actual monarchs, Enrique III and Katherine of Lancaster were betrothed in 1388; Enrique was eight years old and Katherine was fifteen. Enrique did not take the throne until 1393 when he was declared of age.

56. Vega, *Peribáñez y el Comendador de Ocaña*, lines 367–72. Italics added.

57. Vega, *Peribáñez and the Comendador*, lines 2452–55. The translation does not include either variation of "cansados" or "casados."

58. Márquez Villanueva quoted in Vega, *Peribáñez y el Comendador de Ocaña*, 169.

59. Ibid., lines 947–58.

60. Vega, *Peribáñez and the Comendador*, lines 3035–42.

61. See, for example, Lope's *Fuente Ovejuna*, Calderón's *El médico de su honra*, and *El pintor de su deshonra*.

62. Vega, *Peribáñez y el Comendador de Ocaña*, lines 1020–22.

~

CHAPTER THREE

Bad Breath, Impotence, and Poetry as Grounds for Divorce in Cervantes's *El juez de los divorcios*

So marriage has its disappointment—call this its impotence to domesticate sexuality without discouraging it, or its stupidity in the face of the riddle of intimacy, which repels where it attracts, or in the face of the puzzle of ecstasy, which is violent while it is tender, as if the leopard should lie down with the lamb. And the disappointment seeks revenge, a revenge, as it were, for having made one discover one's incompleteness, one's transience, one's homelessness.

—Stanley Cavell, *Pursuits of Happiness: The Hollywood Comedy of Remarriage*

While these words are far removed from the historical time and place in which Cervantes produced his works, "disappointment" and a "desire for revenge" exemplify the actions of the husbands and wives in his fiction. Couples such as Anselmo and Camila from the episode of *El curioso impertinente* in *El ingenioso don Quijote de la Mancha* or Cañizares and Lorenza from exemplary novel, *El viejo extremeño*, hardly constitute the "perfectos casados" prescribed by sixteenth-century treatises espousing the institution of marriage. Rather, these imperfect couples repeatedly test the limits of the conjugal bond to the point that not only is this bond broken, but also their lives are lost in the process. Cervantes's representations of marriage raise numerous questions including the role of free will within the larger social collective body. Does the conjugal bond—considered sacred by the Church—*necessarily* confer social legitimacy to all of its participants? Might marriage actually intensify the sense of "transience" and "homelessness" among the members of a community bound by notions of blood purity and honor? While the subject of blood purity arises in *El juez de los divorcios* just as it does in Lope's *Peribáñez*, Cervantes's interlude casts a far more ironic eye on its ability to guarantee felicitous marital relations.

The recurrence of the marriage theme throughout Cervantine fiction suggests that his works contributed substantially to one of the major controversies of the sixteenth century. In terms of Cervantes's dramatic works, marriage plays a significant role in nearly all of his *entremeses* or interludes, works that Marc Vitse refers to as "abbreviated comedies."[1] As opposed to an idealized image of conjugal harmony, these conflicts result in a more complex vision of the institution. This is particularly the case in *El juez de los divorcios*, the first of the *entremeses*, as it parodies marriage by means of a series of couples that take their turn to plea their grounds for divorce before a judge. In the end, he grants none of them the divorce they desperately seek, thus rendering the title of the play oxymoronic. The following discussion focuses on *El juez de los divorcios* given that it is one of the interludes that best exemplifies many of the central problems of the conjugal bond in Cervantes's works as a whole.

Cervantes was sixteen years old when the Council of Trent (1545–1563) celebrated its twenty-fourth session in 1563. In what would become a turning point in the history of the institution, the Council reaffirmed the sacramental status of the conjugal bond.[2] The Council's declaration on marriage begins with a statement on the presumably permanent as well as the sacred nature of marriage and then goes on to describe its purpose: "The perpetual and indissoluble bond of matrimony was expressed by the first parent of the human race, when, under the influence of the divine Spirit, he said: *This now is bone of my bones and flesh of my flesh. Wherefore a man shall leave father and mother and shall cleave to his wife, and they shall be two in one flesh.* But that by this bond two only are united and joined together."[3] According to this passage, the source of the conjugal bond is sacred, and the exclusive purpose of marriage is procreation. More importantly, this declaration claims that marriage constitutes the *only* means by which to sanction sexual intercourse as exemplified by the statement, "But that by this bond two only are united and joined together." The Council of Trent thus attempted to circumscribe what it considered subversive behavior within clearly defined boundaries by asserting that marriage represents the one and only legitimate means of engaging in sexual intercourse. That the marriage sacrament was taken seriously is illustrated by the Inquisition's persecution of those who did not adhere to Tridentine doctrines by taking action "against numerous individuals who had declared that sex ('simple fornication' in legal terminology) between unmarried individuals was permissible."[4]

The subversive quality of Cervantes's *entremeses* has long been a matter of critical debate. Referring to *El juez de los divorcios*, Stanislav Zimic considers Cervantes's daring in putting into doubt the moral and religious basis of the conjugal bond.[5] In a similar vein, Nicholas Spadaccini specifies that *El juez de los divorcios* explores the socioeconomic as well as the sentimental basis of the marriage contract. María Dolores Bravo Arriaga makes the strongest claim for the play's subversive qualities, by suggesting that it constitutes a "fuerte crítica, desacralizadora, que Cervantes hace de los valores que sustentan la ideología de su tiempo" (strong, desacralizing criticism that Cervantes makes of the values sustaining the ideology of his time).[6] In contrast to these interpretations, in "Burla e ideología en los entremeses" Marc Vitse argues that Cervantes's interludes conform to the ideological imperatives of the period by conforming to a genre that permitted—and even encouraged—satire. Anne J. Cruz follows this line of argument as she describes the "limits" of the *entremeses'* subversive qualities: "Their indeterminacy notwithstanding, the *entremeses* remain, in the end, only partially successful in deferring cultural authority and control."[7] Cruz bases her reasons on the nature of carnival whereby the state offers temporary relief from its own, rigid controls: "by forming part of such carnivalesque rituals as fairs, town festivals, parodies, and farces, all of which appropriate 'low' humor, the interludes offer an institutionalized escape valve, and thus participate fully in social control."[8]

The question of whether Cervantes's interludes subvert or maintain the prevailing social and political order is unlikely to be settled unequivocally. Referring to *El juez de los divorcios*, Mary Gaylord explains that "Attempts to oblige this *entremés* to take a position for or against marriage, or to make a statement of any kind ultimately reach an impasse. . . . As it blocks our interpretive strategies, the play obliges us to see it as a commentary on the difficulties inherent in providing a faithful mirror of the world."[9] It is this very "impasse" that continues to render *El juez de los divorcios* intriguing for its readers. Notwithstanding the interpretive difficulties that this play presents, Cervantes's representation of marriage offers a unique—and contradictory—perspective on one of the most central social and religious institutions in early modern Spain. While these farces do not necessarily put into question the sacramental definition of the conjugal bond, they do suggest the potential conflict that arises from constraining sexual desire.

Marcel Bataillon suggests the stakes involved in such a conflict by explaining that in Cervantes's concept of "Christian marriage," two concepts of marriage are at play, that is, one that defines marriage as a social contract and another that accepts its spiritual or sacramental dimensions:

> El matrimonio es un lazo social. De ahí el interés que la opinión pública pone en el honor o en la deshonra del marido. Por otra parte "en la religión católica el matrimonio es sacramento que sólo se desata con la muerte," a diferencia de otras religiones, en las que "los matrimonios son una manera de concierto o conveniencia como lo es el de alquilar una casa o otra heredad."[10]

> [Marriage is a social bond. Hence, the interest public opinion places on a husband's honor or dishonor. On the other hand, "in the Catholic religion marriage is a sacrament that is only broken by death," in contrast to other religions where marriage constitutes a kind of agreement or convention such as renting a house or other property.]

In this passage, Bataillon cites Periando from *Los trabajos de Persiles y Segismunda*, although the sentiment is echoed in other Cervantine works, most notably in the episode of *El curioso impertinente* in *Don Quixote*.[11] Bataillon suggests that neither the social nor the sacramental definition of marriage prevails in Cervantes's works; rather, the contradiction between the ideal and the real marriage represents the true point of departure.

Cervantes's *entremeses* do not, however, produce a bland neutralization of the conflict between two, distinct views of the conjugal bond. Instead, they dramatize the human dimension of the ongoing battle between both concepts of marriage. In *El juez de los divorcios*, for example, Mariana, the first of three wives to present her grounds for divorce, suggests a radically different definition of marriage than that offered by the Council of Trent:

> En los reinos y en las repúblicas bien ordenadas, había de ser limitado el tiempo de los matrimonios, y en tres años se habían de deshacer o confirmarse de nuevo, como cosas de arrendamiento y no que hayan de durar toda la vida, con perpetuo dolor de entrambas partes.[12]

> [In well-governed kingdoms and republics, marriages should have a time limit, and every three years they should either be dissolved or confirmed anew, like a rent contract; they ought not to last a lifetime, with perpetual grief to both parties.][13]

Whereas the decrees of the Council of Trent insist on the "perpetual and indissoluble bond of matrimony," this wife proposes a far less binding contract. By comparing matrimony with a rental agreement ("cosas de arrendamiento"), her plea for divorce suggests that a legal as well as economic definition of marriage prevail over the sacred dimension emphasized by the Council of Trent.[14] In short, Mariana suggests that connubial bliss is better achieved by making the terms of the marriage "market" more flexible by allowing for divorce, or alternatively, a renewal of the marriage vows.

That Cervantes should employ a woman's voice to redefine marriage in terms that are significantly different than those offered by the Church is perhaps not irrelevant. While Mariana is not the first of Cervantes's characters to put marriage to the test—Anselmo from the *Curioso impertinente* is a notable example—the rhetorical force of her plea to the judge is difficult to ignore: "Señor, ¡divorcio, divorcio, y más divorcio y otras mil veces divorcio!" (Your Honour, divorce, divorce and more divorce, a thousand times divorce!).[15] Her repetitive cry is all the more surprising—and by seventeenth-century standards, heretical—if we consider that the Church denied divorce.[16] To put into question the sacrament of marriage, Cervantes suggests, is to stand on the side of heresy, yet he also adds the possibility that *reason* constitutes the basis of the heretic's demands. After all is said and done, it is *reasonable* to conclude that none of the couples in *El juez de los divorcios* is compatible even if they do not have legal grounds for divorce. Cervantes's fiction asks if it is possible to remain indifferent to women and heretics' voices despite their status as second-class citizens in early modern Spain, when the basis of their arguments is rational. Cervantes's *entremeses* remind us that religious faith as well as marital fidelity does not necessarily depend on reason. In fact, faith and fidelity may actually work to undermine reason, just as skepticism and infidelity can represent equally corrosive forces in a society where religious doctrines are not open to question.[17]

Despite the very emotional tone of Mariana's plea, she does not advocate that marriage be contracted on the basis of mutual affection, an opinion that many in the sixteenth century—including the participants of the Council of Trent—were likely to share. This is especially true if we consider the manner in which the decrees of the Council of Trent subordinate erotic desire to the exclusive purpose of procreation. However, while the wives in *El juez de los divorcios* do not sentimentalize marriage, they do express dissatisfaction with their husbands' inability or refusal to perform their conjugal duties. Among the husbands in *El juez de los divorcios*, there exists a sense of impotence in the face of their wives' sexual energy, or in Mary Gaylord's words, "the unsuccessfully repressed female desire which strains on the yoke of matrimony."[18] The eroticizing of conjugal relations on the part of the wives—as opposed to the sentimentalizing of said relations—suggests a view of matrimony that is unique to the early modern period.

In keeping with Mariana's call to renew the marriage contract every three years, Sebastian de Covarrubias's definition of the word *casado* (husband) in his *Tesoro de la lengua castellana o española* (1611) focuses on its etymological root *casa* (house), that is, the kind of space that may be rented, bought, or sold: "El que ha contrahido matrimonio, porque luego le obligan a poner casa" (One who has contracted marriage because they are obliged to set up a home).[19] Although Covarrubias's dictionary does not constitute a guide to the married life in the strict sense of the word, it is by its very nature a prescriptive text in that it dictates the use of language, including those terms that bear significant relation to conjugal relations. As such, *Tesoro de la lengua castellana o española* offers an invaluable window to the way in which a word such as "husband" was understood in seventeenth-century Spain. In this case, Covarrubias's definition strays considerably from its initial entry cited above in order to provide numerous—and suggestive—derivations of the word *casa*:

Al nombre de casa, se suele añadir calidad de habitación particular, como casa de oración, casa de religión, casa de provocación, casa professa, casa de moneda, casa de contratación, casa pública, casa de posadas, casa de campo, casa de juego, que no se debía permitir, ni disimular, como en los lugares no se permite. Casa pública, la de las ruines mugeres, permitida por evitar mayor mal, y no por esso dexa de ser malo el usar dellas. . . . Solón, para divertir a la juventud de los adulterios e ilegítimos ayuntamientos con la matronas y doncellas del pueblo de Atenas, hizo fuera de la ciudad casa pública, y compró mugeres forasteras de buen parecer y gracia que residiessen en ella y hiciesen buena acogida a los mancebos.[20]

[To the word house, that of a particular kind of abode is usually added, such as a house of prayer, a religious house, a house of provocation, a house for professing vows, a house for minting currency, a house for making contracts, a public house, a resting house, a country home, a gambling house—which should not be allowed or hidden and should remain forbidden—a public house for fallen women, allowed in order to avoid a greater evil, although this should not be a reason to use them. . . . In order to distract young men from adulterous and illegitimate liaisons with Athen's matrons and maidens, Solon constructed a public house outside the city and bought beautiful and charming women to reside in them in order to welcome said young men.]

As in the wife's metaphor of marriage as *cosas de arrendamiento*, Covarrubias's definition of *casado* emphasizes the impersonal elements of domestic space over the affective ties that might bind one in marriage. This etymology also pays a great deal of attention to the economic exchange associated with the *casa de moneda, casa de juego,* and above all, the *casa pública,* or bordello. Given that the Council of Trent allowed for sexual intercourse only within the confines of marriage, as well as the overall distrust of sexual behavior that such controls imply, it is perhaps not surprising that Covarrubias includes both marriage and prostitution in his definition of the word "husband." Although Covarrubias's definition of *casado* condemns prostitution, it also contains an implicit tolerance for it as a means of safeguarding against "worse ills." These ills, Covarrubias suggests, include adultery and illicit intercourse with virgins, activities that presumably profane the sanctity of marriage. By this definition, marriage represents a burden that obligates men to settle down ("le *obligan* a poner casa") thus losing the freedom conventionally associated with bachelorhood. As is characteristic of the *Tesoro,* this work authorizes its definition of the word *casado* by drawing on a body of classical knowledge, in this case, the works of Plutarch that narrate Solon's life. If the Romans sanctioned prostitution in order to protect their virgins and matrons, so the argument goes, then surely modern-day Spaniards could continue doing the same.

While Covarrubias's definition of marriage may have some points in common with the views expressed in *El juez de los divorcios,* there also exist significant differences between them. Cervantes provides a forum for husbands to voice their complaints and for their wives to do the same, whereas Covarrubias fails to recognize the role of wives. The definition of *casado* neither mentions the female spouse, nor does it include a separate entry for them. In *El juez de los divorcios,* moreover, each of the wives is in clear possession of her voice. All three wives who present their case before the judge refer either directly or indirectly to their husband's inability to perform his conjugal duties: either he is too old, too drunk or too distracted to give his wife the attention she demands. It is arguably the dynamic nature of the dispute between husbands *and* wives that lend such vitality to this interlude. At the beginning of *El juez de los divorcios,* for example, the judge asks Mariana to specify her grounds for divorce, to which she responds:

> El ivierno de mi marido, y la primavera de mi edad; el quitarme el sueño, por levantarme a media noche a calentar paños y saquillos de salvado para ponerle en la ijada; el ponerle, ora aquesto, ora aquella ligadura, que ligado le vea yo a un palo por justicia; el cuidado que tengo de ponerle de noche alta cabecera de la cama, jarabes lenitivos, porque no se ahogue del pecho; y el estar obligada a sufrirle el mal olor de la boca, que le güele mal a tres tiros de arcabuz.[21]

[My husband's winter and the springtime of my age. I lose sleep getting up at midnight to heat cloths and bran sacks to lay on the small of his back; I put a truss on him first in one place and then in another—I hope to see him trussed to a stake, and serve him right! I have to prop up his pillow nights, and mix cough syrups to relieve his asthma; and I have to stand his foul breath that you can smell a mile away.][22]

Not only must Mariana suffer her husband's old age and poor health, but also his very bad breath, arguments that the lawyer actually supports:

Pues ley hay que dice, según he oído decir, que por sólo el mal olor de la boca se puede desc[as]ar la mujer del marido, y el marido de la mujer.[23]

[There is in fact a law, as I have heard, that bad breath is a sufficient cause of divorce either in husband or wife.][24]

In a bravura performance that Mariana constructs on the basis of opposites as primordial as winter and spring, she marks the differences that separate her from her husband. Erasmus characterizes marriage as part of the natural order nearly a century before Cervantes's play, while Mariana counters that marriage can function as part of an equally natural *disorder*. While the seriousness of her plea degenerates into a petty complaint about bad breath, this focus on women's desires also represents a significant departure from Covarrubias's definition. In Melveena McKendrick's words, Cervantes's satire makes room for both "inadequate husband and harridan wife."[25] In the context of an *entremés* such as *El viejo celoso*, where the *senex*'s age actually triples that of his wife, the tenor of the young wife's complaints in *El juez de los divorcios* are all the more compelling. Moreover, the reader-spectator of Cervantes's play is not likely to take the lawyer's precedent for bad breath seriously, allowing for the satire to extend beyond the complaint of a single, female plaintiff to the legal establishment as a whole that has become decrepit in much the same way as her husband.[26]

Like Mariana, the other wives who present their cases before the judge insinuate their husband's inability or lack of interest in performing their conjugal duties. According to Guiomar, the second wife to plead her case before the judge, her husband does little to find gainful employment and instead spends his days in the less lucrative activities of gambling and gossiping. At night, moreover, she blames poetry as the primary culprit for her husband's reduced libido:

vuelve a media noche; cena si lo halla; y si no, santíguase, bosteza y acuéstase; y en toda la noche no sosiega dando vueltas. Pregúntole qué tiene. Respóndeme que está haciendo un soneto en la memoria para un amigo que se le ha pedido; y da en ser poeta, como si fuese oficio con quien no estuviese vinculada la necesidad del mundo.[27]

[he . . . returns at midnight, sups if he finds anything to eat, and if not, crosses himself, yawns and goes to bed. All night long he flops about, not quiet a minute. I ask him what's the matter; he answers that he is composing a sonnet in his mind for a friend who asked him for one; he persists in being a poet, as though it were not the most impecunious profession in the whole world.][28]

Guiomar's complaint not only makes plain her frustration, but also her disdain for her husband's pursuit of poetry, particularly in times of economic necessity. She does this by characterizing her husband's nightly ritual, detailing the moment in which he makes the sign of the cross, yawns, and falls asleep—hardly the stuff of sexual arousal. His true passion revolves around poetry; he forsakes his most basic needs for the sake of verse, including eating and sleeping, not to speak of other, more carnal pleasures. Given that Cervantes himself was a poet, it is unlikely that he would share Guiomar's disapproval of her husband's pastimes. Her description of her husband's inadequacy thus represents an ironic gesture characteristic of Cervantine fiction as a whole.

Just as marriage plays a role in relation to blood purity during Spain's early modern period, so too Cervantes's works dramatize the values the institution of marriage is presumed to uphold—values that were clearly constructed on the basis of excluding the *converso* community. While the stigma of a *converso* past was eradicated with difficulty in sixteenth- and seventeenth-century Spain, matrimonial alliances could weaken ties to a Jewish lineage. Similarly, *converso* blood, as well as infidelity on the wife's part constituted two of the chief sources of social stigma during this period. Initially considered a positive quality, honor becomes oppressive at the moment society calls upon the individual to safeguard values over which little control is possible: "el individuo está considerado como portador de los valores esenciales de la vida colectiva y que, de este modo, cuando es confrontado con un caso de honor, se convierte en intérpete de unas fuerzas superiores a él" (The individual is considered as holding the essential values of the collective life and so when faced with a case of honor, becomes an interpreter of forces greater than that individual).[29]

Cervantes's *entremeses* suggest that marriage and *limpieza de sangre* also depend on individuals to interpret social values that are defined at a collective level. The act of interpretation is, however, subjective, and Cervantes's characters come into conflict at the moment definitions of self must conform to broader prerogatives. Nowhere is this conflict more apparent than when the characters voice their views on sexuality and race. In *El juez de los divorcios*, for example, the judge represents the collective will as embodied by the law, whereas the husbands and wives represent the individual desire for freedom from the bonds that join them in matrimony. These two clash and there appears little possibility of reconciliation between individual desire and collective will over the course of the action.

One may ask whether the separation these couples ultimately seek is not, in fact, from the judge himself who represents the political and economic interests of the state. By postponing any further judgment on the cases until they are put in writing at the conclusion of the interlude, the judge contributes to the bureaucratization of a legal system whose principal beneficiaries are himself, the lawyers, and the notaries. He actually recognizes the validity of the plaintiff's claims only to deny them: "aunque algunos de los aquí estáis habéis dado algunas causas que traen aparejada sentencia de divorcio, con todo eso, es menester que conste por escrito" (although some of you who are here have adduced reasons sufficient for divorce, none the less it must all be set in writing).[30] In the judge's opinion, writing—that is, the material manifestation of the word—takes precedence over the more temporal qualities of oral performance, no matter how impressive this performance may be. The judge's demand that the cases be put in writing displaces the plaintiff's pleas for divorce; similarly, writing represents the very antithesis of a dramatic performance. This demand dramatizes the *act* of writing and constitutes a reminder of the written dimension of the marriage vow reiterated by the Council of Trent. In this final—and thus highly charged moment of the interlude—the judge suggests that what has been accomplished in writing can only be undone in writing.

Of the plaintiff's performances, one of the most outstanding comes from the third plaintiff's, a surgeon who gives his four "reasons" for divorce:

> La primera, porque no la puedo ver más que a todos los diablos; la segunda, por lo que ella se sabe; la tercera, por lo que yo me callo; la cuarta, porque no me lleven los demonios, cuando desta vida vaya, si he de durar en su compañía hasta mi muerte.[31]

> [First, because I can't bear the sight of her more than of all the devils in hell; second, for a reason she knows; third, for one that I don't care to tell; forth, because I hope demons may fly away with me when I die, if I will remain in her company for the rest of my life.][32]

These words reveal more by what they do *not* say than what they do say. A masterful performance on the part of the surgeon his "speech-act" projects domestic conflict better than any reference to his wife's specific trespasses.[33] This passage simultaneously represents an indictment, a demand, and an insult, as the surgeon enumerates his grounds for divorce without explicitly referring to them. The sharp contrast between the order he imposes on language and the opaque quality of this same language serves to draw as well as deflect attention from his plea. But it is precisely this contradiction that may defeat his purpose. Such a verbal strategy suggests that this husband is compelled to identify his reasons for divorce indirectly because they represent a source of public humiliation, very likely a slight on his honor in the form of his wife's infidelity. As in *Peribáñez*, cuckoldry, whether realized or not, proves to be a source of shame so powerful that the characters cannot even refer to it directly, much less name it. What distinguishes *El juez de los divorcios*, however, is that this shame gives rise to hilarity—the spectator can never be sure *what*, in fact, the surgeon is talking about, much less his "reasons" for divorce.

The final case to appear before the judge reveals the limitations of marriage as an institution that presumably guarantees social legitimacy. This case belongs to a husband who arrives alone because his wife is far too contentious to appear in the courtroom. As the final plaintiff to appear before the judge, he is perhaps the most significant of the four cases. This husband refers to himself as a *ganapán* and *cristiano viejo*, assignations that are presumably designed to lend greater weight to his plea for divorce. The *ganapán* or porter confesses his affinity for alcohol as well as the dimensions of his sacrifice in the hands of a *mujer errada* whom he married while under the influence:

> Señor juez: ganapán soy, no lo niego, pero cristiano viejo, y hombre de bien a las derechas; y, si no fuese que alguna vez me tomo del vino, o él me toma a mí, que es lo más cierto, ya hubiera sido prioste en la confradía de los hermanos de la carga. . . . Quiero que sepa el señor juez que, estando una vez muy enfermo de los vaguidos de Baco, prometí de casarme con una mujer errada. Volví en mí, sané, y cumplí la promesa, y caséme con una mujer que saqué de pecado . . . ha salido tan soberbia y de tan mala condición, que nadie llega a su tabla con quien no riña, . . . y los deshonra hasta la cuarta generación, sin tener hora de paz con todas sus vecinas ya parleras.[34]

> [Your Honor, I'm only a street-porter, I admit, but I am a Christian of pure blood and a straight and honorable man; and if it weren't for my taking a drop of wine now and then (or its taking me, which is nearer the truth), I would have manager of the Charcoal-Carriers Union. . . . I would have Your Honour

know that once when I was under the influence I promised to marry a woman
of the street. When I came to, I recovered my reason and kept my promise and
married this woman whom I took from a life of vice . . . she has turned out
so arrogant and ill-tempered that she quarrels with everyone who approaches
her stand . . . and she insults their ancestry back to the fourth generation, and
never has an hour's peace with any of her neighbors and partners.][35]

Rather than bestow social legitimacy on the porter, marriage brings him
public shame. Moreover, his reference to his credentials as a *cristiano viejo*
(old Christian) stands in contrast to the dishonor brought upon him by his
"errant" wife. She is errant in both senses of the word for if in the past she
strayed sexually in her life as a prostitute, in the present, she escapes the
confines of the domestic abode to which wives were typically relegated in the
early modern period in order to occupy the public space of the market. But
perhaps most telling of all in the porter's speech is the simultaneous mention
of both blood purity and marriage, as if one guaranteed the other. Cervantes
parodies this assumption by presenting the flawed logic of such an argument
in the voice of a drunkard. The porter's plea suggests that neither marriage
nor blood purity serve to confer social legitimacy—in this case, marriage
serves to intensify his isolation.

The action of *El juez de los divorcios* is predicated on undoing what has
already been done, that is, taking back what has already been said. Is it
possible for the judge to acknowledge promises that have been made while
simultaneously rendering them null and void? The judge does not find
grounds for divorce based on any of the reasons offered by the plaintiffs.
These causes provide a clue as to the kind of reasoning that prevails in the
entremés as a whole. From the opening scene onward, the verbal exchanges
in *El juez de los divorcios* generate an unconventional logic that may be
best described as nonsense that is in turn compounded by the musicians'
entrance at the conclusion of the play. As they burst into the courtroom,
they extend an invitation to the judge to celebrate the reconciliation of
a couple that had formerly sought a divorce. It is telling that this happy
couple never appears on stage, and as such, their case lacks the dramatic
force of the previous cases.

The refrain to the musicians' song, "*que vale el peor concierto / más que
el divorcio mejor*" (*for reconcilement, even the worst, is better than the best
divorce*), claims that no matter how valid the reasons, reconciliation is
preferable to separation. But is it, even by sixteenth-century standards?
Such an argument clashes with the couples' pleas for divorce and leads
Stansilav Zimic to ask how one reconciles the musicians' advice with the

"ferocious" relations that the court proceedings prove once and again to be completely irreconcilable.[36] The answer, Cervantes suggests in *El juez de los divorcios*, is that there is very little likelihood that the musicians' advice will improve the marital lives of the couples, and that separation is, in fact, preferable to prolonging the agony of their incompatibility. The musicians' refrain therefore stands as a profoundly ironic statement on those powers that deny separation regardless of the circumstances. If a "happy ending" demands a happy marriage as is the case in so many comedies in early modern Spain, then Cervantes may also be casting an ironic glance at the formulaic demands of such works. The musicians' harmony in fact underscores the conjugal discord that constitutes the prevailing tone in the judge's divorce court.

In *El juez de los divorcios*, the conjugal yoke intensifies the couple's desperation rather than draw them together in any physical or emotional sense. Tridentine marriage, Cervantes suggests, forces the individual to seek redress from the confines of domestic space in the most public of forums, that is, the courtroom. The institution of marriage also exacerbates the very conflict it is presumed to resolve: instead of restraining sexual desire it provokes it. And just as importantly, the matrimonial conflicts in *El juez de los divorcios* bring attention to other, seemingly unrelated tensions afflicting Spanish society during the period, namely the obsession with blood purity and honor. These issues are not exclusive to *El juez de los divorcios*, but reappear in significant ways in nearly all of Cervantes's *entremeses* including *El rufián viudo llamado Trampagos*, *La guarda cuidadosa*, *El viejo celoso*, *La cueva de Salamanca*, and *El retablo de las maravillas*.[37]

In the context of Cervantes's *entremeses*, illegitimacy and *converso* origins represent two of the greatest sources of public contempt in early modern Spain. These are not exclusive categories, but rather bear an intimate connection to each other. Neither fidelity nor faith, Cervantes suggests, are absolute values, despite the national obsession to pursue and persecute those who trespass against them. To profess either fidelity or faith in absolute terms may result in an impressive—and hilarious—verbal performance in a court of law, but such declarations may be ineffectual in achieving their ends. Nonetheless, the court of law is an argueably effective vehicle in preventing the hostilities between the spouses from escalating further into physical violence, at least when the couples are in the presence of the judge. In many ways, the absence of physical violence allows for *El juez de los divorcios* to maintain its comic tone throughout the action. As we will see in the following chapter, the absence of an effective political outlet for resolving spousal conflict results in tragedy.

Notes

1. Vitse, "Burla e ideología en los entremeses," 166.
2. Brundage, *Law, Sex, and Christian Society in Medieval Europe*, 563–65, 574–75.
3. Schroeder, *Canons and Decrees of the Council of Trent*, 180.
4. Kagan and Dyer, *Inquisitorial Inquiries*, 8.
5. Zimic, "La ejemplaridad de los entremeses de Cervantes," 451.
6. Bravo Arriaga, "Los entremeses cervantinos, valores sociales y risa crítica: *El retablo de las maravillas*," 142.
7. Cruz, "Deceit, Desire, and the Limits of Subversion in Cervantes's Interludes," 120.
8. Ibid., 122.
9. Gaylord, "The Order in the Court," 84.
10. Bataillon, *Varia lección de clásicos españoles*, 245.
11. For example, in the episode of the *Curioso impertinente* in *Don Quixote*, Lotario attempts to dissuade Anselmo from testing his wife's fidelity by emphasizing the sacramental nature of marriage: "entonces fue instituido el divino sacramento del matrimonio con tales lazos, que sola la muerte puede desatarlos. Y tiene tanta fuerza y virtud este milagroso sacramento, que hace que dos diferentes personas sean una mesma carne; y aun hace más en los buenos casados, que, aunque tienen dos almas, no tienen más de una voluntad" (Then was instituted the divine sacrament of matrimony, whose bonds only death can untie. This miraculous sacrament has such strength and virtue that it makes two different persons one single flesh; and with happily married couples it does even more, for though they have two souls, they have but a single will). Cervantes Saavedra, *El ingenioso hidalgo don Quijote de la Mancha*, 411; Cervantes Saavedra, *Don Quixote*, 336. This definition of marriage virtually replicates that of the Council of Trent.
12. Cervantes Saavedra, *Entremeses*, 98.
13. Cervantes Saavedra, *The Interludes of Cervantes*, 3–5.
14. Anne J. Cruz comments on the economic motivation for Mariana's plea: "in her grievance against the perpetuity of marriage vows, Mariana's own discourse becomes allied with the increasing commodification of religious rituals." Cruz, "Deceit, Desire, and the Limits of Subversion in Cervantes's Interludes," 127.
15. Cervantes Saavedra, *Entremeses*, 98; Cervantes Saavedra, *The Interludes of Cervantes*, 3.
16. "The problem that divorce presented was hardly discussed in Trent due to a Protestant thesis that, by rejecting Rome's matrimonial jurisprudence and its causes for annulment, allowed for remarriage after repudiating an adulterous wife. This thesis was condemned." Bataillon, *Varia lección de clásicos españoles*, 248.
17. Lotario, in the episode of *El curioso impertinente* also raises the question of heresy at the moment that his friend asks him to test his wife's fidelity: "tienes tú ahora el ingenio como el que siempre tienen los moros, a los cuales no se les puede dar a entender el error de su secta con las acotaciones de la Santa Escritura, ni con razones

que consistan en especulación del entendimiento, ni que vayan fundadas en artículos de fe, sino que les han de traer ejemplos palpables, fáciles, inteligibles, demonstrativos, indubitables, con demonstraciones matemáticas que no se pueden negar" (Your attitude of mind, Anselmo, seems to me to be the same as that of the Moors, who cannot be convinced of the errors of their sect by quotations from Holy Scripture or by arguments derived from speculations or founded on the canons of faith, but one must have examples that are simple, palpable, intelligible, and indubitable, with irrefutable mathematical proofs). Cervantes Saavedra, *El ingenioso hidalgo don Quijote de la Mancha*, 405; Cervantes Saavedra, *Don Quixote*, 331.

18. Gaylord, "The Order in the Court," 86.

19. Covarrubias, *Tesoro de la lengua castellana o española*, 314.

20. Ibid.

21. Cervantes Saavedra, *Entremeses*, 99.

22. Cervantes Saavedra, *The Interludes of Cervantes*, 5.

23. Cervantes Saavedra, *Entremeses*, 99.

24. Cervantes Saavedra, *The Interludes of Cervantes*, 5.

25. McKendrick, "Writings for the Stage," 152.

26. "The target of Cervantine satire does not consist primarily of the unhappy couples, but of the religious and administrative institution that through its dogmatic rigidity is determined to keep them together without reason." Zimic, "La ejemplaridad de los entremeses de Cervantes," 451.

27. Cervantes Saavedra, *Entremeses*, 103–4.

28. Cervantes Saavedra, *The Interludes of Cervantes*, 11.

29. Bennassar, *Los españoles*, 196.

30. Cervantes Saavedra, *Entremeses*, 109.

31. Ibid., 107.

32. Cervantes Saavedra, *The Interludes of Cervantes*, 15.

33. Austin, *How to Do Things with Words*, 1–11. These pages include a discussion of the particular nature of matrimonial promises as speech-acts.

34. Cervantes Saavedra, *Entremeses*, 108.

35. Cervantes Saavedra, *The Interludes of Cervantes*, 17.

36. "How does one reconcile this advice with the fierce marital relations (true 'portable hell' as Quevedo would call them) that the play presents as absolutely irreconcilable?" Zimic, "La ejemplaridad de los entremeses de Cervantes," 450.

37. *El retablo de las maravillas* represents an especially extraordinary example of the ways in which marriage fails to alleviate the social and sexual tensions, and may, in fact, make them worse. The *gobernador* of a rural village agrees that a three-person troupe give a dramatic performance in celebration of his goddaughter's wedding. The *pícaros* or con-artists constituting this diminutive troupe set out to swindle the villagers by placing two conditions for viewing the "marvels" contained in their performance: blood purity and having been born in wedlock. As in *El juez de los divorcios*, faith and fidelity become interconnected concerns as well as the basis of a collective neurosis. Not only do the performers dupe their audience into

applauding a performance that never takes place, but they also raise the stakes by putting into question the bride's reputation before she has contracted marriage. The audience's failure to recognize the swindlers' deception suggests their blind faith in the social institutions presumably designed to confer legitimacy. Rather than bind their community, marriage serves to aggravate their anxieties, as well as the sense of "homelessness" and "transience" mentioned at the beginning of this discussion.

CHAPTER FOUR

A Question of Honor

Marriage and Murder in Pedro Calderón de la Barca's El médico de su honra

While comic works for the stage in Spain's early modern period tend to end in marriage, many tragedies do just the reverse: they begin in marriage and conclude in the presence of the wife's dead body. The striking, bloodstained appearance of this body at the conclusion of the drama represents the final sign of suffering—words cannot match the visual impact of her corpse. This presence is not, however, the only sign of tragedy, for the wife's appearance in the opening scenes of the drama acts as a prophetic sign of doom.[1] Her death at the hand of her husband represents the destruction of the conjugal bond and of the promise on which this bond rests. As the action unfolds, the husband perceives his wife's betrayal that as a result puts into question his honor. As a consequence of this conviction, he murders her, severing the conjugal bond in the most violent way possible. Unlike comedy, the mistakes tragic protagonists commit cannot be redeemed, since the potential for violence is fully realized. The husband in these dramas may remarry, as does Gutierre in *El médico de su honra* and Juan Roca in *El pintor de su deshonra*, both works by Pedro Calderón de la Barca. However, these engagements in the final moments of the drama do not hold the promise of a new beginning as they do in the comedy. On the contrary, they suggest the grim repetition of an endless cycle of violence.

Calderón's wife-murder plays introduce serious questions about the values on which marriage was based in the sixteenth and seventeenth centuries. These values correspond to a complex network of social relations bound by a strict hierarchical order in which women play roles secondary to those of men, slaves are subordinated to their masters, and all are subject to the absolute power of the monarch. In Ruth El Saffar's words, "The universe that Calderón's characters inhabit is one in which only hierarchy preserves the order, a hierarchy which has, ultimately, to be preserved for its own sake."[2] Therefore, the tragedy of a dramatic work such as *El médico de su honra* cannot be reduced to the private conflict between spouses, although it is rooted in their original conjugal contract. In this regard, it is difficult to exaggerate the importance of the concept of honor in this and other works where marital strife plays a central role. According to Bartolomé Bennassar, honor is the concept or "passion" that best defines the Spanish drama of the period where, in its most positive incarnation, it represents an individual's self-esteem, a "peculiar form of pride," and, at its worst, acts as an incontrollable force that subjects the individual to extreme degradation.[3]

Scholarship of Calderón's wife-murder plays has long been divided on the question of whether these works uphold or critique the honor code, although more recent criticism suggests a more ambivalent view.[4] Perhaps nowhere is the question of honor more problematic than in *El médico de su honra* due to the extreme violence to which the main protagonist recurs in order to maintain his reputation. Given the sanction of the wife's murder by the King at the conclusion, it is not possible to state that this drama takes an unequivocal stand against upholding honor at all costs. On the other hand, a close reading of *El médico* suggests a more critical view of the tragic consequences involved in placing such a high value on honor, particularly where conjugal relations are concerned.

In *El médico*, language plays a central role in the construction of the promise of marriage, which in turn sustains the social order. Power represents a deciding factor in who is allowed to speak and when, from the King who demands that his subjects speak or keep silent, to the *gracioso* who refuses to utter his name. In Roberto González Echevarría's analysis of *La vida es sueño*, he points out that conflict does not lead to "impoverishment, but, on the contrary, a linguistic enrichment that arises from incompatibility."[5] The same may be said for the protagonists of *El médico* where their difficulty with language does not represent linguistic "impoverishment," but rather represents marital conflict or "incompatibility." Accordingly, *El médico* dramatizes the perils of language and the promises words make or fail to keep. Words may appear wedded to their speakers, but *El médico* renders the marriage between speaker and word illusory.

Throughout *El médico*, words fail the protagonists at precisely the moment they most need to articulate their pain or fear, and their subsequent inability to speak produces even greater anxiety. Language becomes a source of anguish as troubling as the suffering itself. When Gutierre suspects that the King's brother, Enrique, has been courting his wife, he searches in vain to express his suffering; "No sé cómo signifique / mi pena; turbado estoy."[6] His confusion intensifies in the same scene when he adds:

No sé como lo diga;
que no hay voz que signifique
una cosa, que no sea
un átomo indivisible.[7]

[I do not well know how to signify
My grievance][8]

The convoluted grammar of this passage, which is lost in translation, creates a sense of the linguistic abyss at whose edge Gutierre stands; for example, the triple repetition of "que" subordinates one meaning to another until it is all but obscure. Unable to "signify" his pain, he is incapable of alleviating his suffering. Throughout the drama, Gutierre searches, reads, and interprets conflicting signs of marital betrayal, but ultimately rejects their contradictions. As such, he resists words' inherent heterogeneity, and he searches for a one-to-one correspondence between words and their meanings, just as he desires for Mencía to be indivisible unto himself. When Gutierre asks her, "¿Puede en los dos / haber engaño, si en vos / quedo yo, y vos vais en mí?" (But how can there be treachery when I / Remain in you, and you go forth in me?) he emphasizes his belief in conjugal indivisibility.[9] However, as the protagonists acknowledge throughout the drama, words and people possess a history and life of their own; they may be remembered or forgotten, but their heterogeneous meanings prevail over their homogeneity. The control Gutierre exercises over his own voice is therefore limited by the very nature of language.

In the passages cited above, the King's presence and the delicate, political nature of Gutierre's complaint against the monarch's brother suggests that Gutierre's linguistic difficulties have more to do with the superior status of his interlocutor than with any inherent incompetence on Gutierre's part. However, his desire to reduce language to its simplest common dominator is present even when he finds himself alone:

Ya estoy solo, ya bien puedo
hablar. ¡Ay Dios!, quién supiera
reducir solo a un discurso,
medir con solo una idea

tantos géneros de agravios
tantos linajes de penas
como cobardes me asaltan,
como atrevidos me cercan.[10]

[Now I'm alone, I can speak out loud.
O God, if only by a single speech,
And by one sole idea, I could dispose
Of all these cowardly and daring foes,
These generations, lineages, and breeds
Of outrages, and injuries, and woes,
Who both assault me and besiege me too!][11]

Expressions such as "reducir" and "medir" reveal Gutierre's attempt to impose order on language. The conflict Gutierre expresses here does not concern a search for a new language or new meanings; rather, unable to find the right words, he advocates repressing language altogether by privileging silence. The tragic consequences of this repression culminate in his permanent silencing of Mencía by means of murder. Given this startling conclusion, it is worth considering the nature of Gutierre's suffering. The expressions, "linajes de penas" and "géneros de agravios," suggest an underlying concern with sexuality in terms of the reproduction engendering a family line or lineage. These definitions suggest that Gutierre is as obsessed with the number of problems that overwhelm him, as he is by their source that, in this case, is Mencía.

Although Mencía expresses a problematic relationship to speech, her difficulty is of an altogether different nature. Gutierre cannot find the words he needs to articulate his suffering and therefore seeks to place strict limitations on discourse. Mencía, on the other hand, searches for an opportunity to simply *speak*. Her anguish is produced by her desire to break the silence which surrounds her past and present.[12] This desire becomes particularly acute when the past erupts in the present as when she sees Enrique, a former suitor, in the opening scene. Whereas Gutierre wonders how he might simplify his confusion with a few simple words, Mencía cries,

¡O quién pudiera, ah, cielos,
con licencia de su honor
hacer aquí sentimientos!
¡O quién pudiera dar voces,
y romper con el silencio
cárceles de nieve, donde
Está aprisionado el fuego

que ya, resuelto en cenizas,
es ruina que está diciendo:
"Aquí fue amor"![13]

[Heavens! Could I but give way
To my great grief, and yet respect my honour!
Could I but cry out my sorrow, jointly breaking
The silence and this prison, here, of snow,
Which is my breast! Its prisoner was once
A fire, which now has been reduced to cinders,
Whose ruined ash proclaims: "This, once, was Love."][14]

Here Mencía laments not having honor's license to acknowledge her past, even though this past is presumably buried in ashes. Petrarchan images of fire and snow are linked to those of speech and silence; for instance, the metaphorical prison of snow guards a secret consisting of a fire that has long been extinguished. Only its charred remains stand as a monument to Mencía's past, and this monument identifies the fire as a former love. These images of prisons and ruins evoke allegorical spaces of desolation and despair from which Mencía is unable to escape. Contrary to Gutierre, she represents silence as a repressive force pervading an isolated psychological landscape.[15] Mencía represents her isolation not only in temporal but also spatial terms. Progressive tenses ("está aprisionado," "está diciendo") project a sense of movement in the present that stands in stark contrast to the past ("Aquí fue amor"). These temporal changes not only represent a grammatical shift but also create contradictions Mencía attempts to resolve in vain. The change from fire to ashes suggests the power of time to diminish desire, although the metaphorical "ruins" emerging from these ashes stand as testimony to the power of love to withstand the ravages of time. Mencía's present conjugal status prevents her from recovering this past. This is, in part, her tragedy: her beloved has arrived too late.[16]

If Mencía's desire is part of an irrevocable past, one might ask why she goes to such lengths to name it. In part, she recognizes that her ontological status depends on a past she cannot or will not forget and that her history, like many histories, is materialized through the word. Shortly after Gutierre leaves her in order to greet the King upon his arrival in Seville, Mencía confides in her slave,

Nací en Sevilla, y en ella
me vio Enrique, festejó
mis desdenes, celebró

mi nombre, ¡felice estrella!
Fuese, y mi padre atropella
la libertad que hubo en mí.
La mano a Gutierre di,
volvió Enrique, y en rigor,
tuve amor, y tengo honor;
esto es cuanto sé de mí.[17]

[In Seville I was born, and there
Henry first saw me, thawed my cold disdain
With living praise—O happy Star!—and then
He went away on duty. When my father
Cut short the liberty I once enjoyed,
To put me in a convent, as I feared,—
I gave my hand to Don Gutierre. Then
Henry returned. I love him: yet my honour
Forbids. That's all I know about myself.][18]

In this highly abridged autobiography, Mencía gives voice to the most relevant events of her past. She reduces her history to ten short lines by contrasting the joys of her courtship in which Enrique celebrated her name with the imposition of paternal authority. Her reference to her lost liberty reveals that she did not, in fact, consent to marry Gutierre. This revelation has serious consequences for the course of the action, because she is bound to Gutierre by a conjugal promise that she did not make but which was nevertheless imposed on her.[19] Such a promise is doomed to failure, because the premise on which it is made is faulty from the start. Paternal authority usurps Mencía's freedom to give or withdraw her consent to a promise of marriage. The imperfect conditions in which Mencía and Gutierre originally contract the conjugal promise lead to necessarily disastrous results.

In *El médico* the protagonists often employ figurative language as an alternative to repressing language altogether.[20] Rhetorical figures such as metaphor or irony permit the protagonists to speak the unspeakable. For example, in the first act, before Enrique makes his exit, he says to himself, "Estáse Troya ardiendo, / y Eneas de mis sentidos, / he de librarlos del fuego" (All Troy / Is burning here, and I, Aeneas-like, / Must save my burning senses from the fire!)[21] Troy's political downfall as the result of a conjugal transgression stands as the metaphoric expression of Enrique's overwhelming desire for another man's wife. It will only be in retrospect, however, that the implications of these words will be fully appreciated by the spectator. The reference to Troy will take on greater significance in the course of the action, since it will reflect the political dimensions of the personal conflict; Enrique's disruption of Gutierre and Mencía's conjugal harmony holds serious consequences in the court of his brother the King. Still, Enrique's metaphor serves to create dramatic suspense, since only the course of events will reveal the identity of the names he dares not mention directly.

While figurative language enables the protagonists to give voice to their suffering, constant recourse to tropes such as metaphor also present serious difficulties in *El médico*. Above all, it prevents Mencía as well as Gutierre from identifying the primary cause of their conflict. Unable to name the problem, they are unable to find its solution. As Francisco Ruiz Ramón observes, metaphorical language may, in fact, aggravate conflict: "the 'fire-ashes-ruins' metaphor with which Doña Mencía tries to exorcise the force of Eros, distancing it into the past, has the contrary effect: instead of distancing Eros, it brings it closer. Instead of extinguishing the fire, it lights it."[22] Throughout *El médico*, the distinction between the literal and figurative is blurred to such a degree that it becomes difficult, if not impossible to distinguish between them. For example, when Mencía inquires about Enrique's health when he is first thrown off his horse and arrives at her door, he replies, "Estoy tan bueno, / que nunca estuve mejor; / sólo en esta pierna siento / un dolor" (Never so well; excepting for this leg).[23] What exactly is the nature of Enrique's pain? Is it produced by the fall from his horse or by something else? A long literary tradition that links physical pain to erotic desire supports an alternative interpretation. Nonetheless, the inherent ambiguity of language does not permit us to conclude whether Enrique is speaking literally or figuratively.

The drama's title announces its guiding metaphor before the action even begins. Despite the title of physician that Gutierre assigns himself, he does not heal anybody or anything, a point that Bruce W. Wardropper summarizes by stating that "real physicians kill by accident; Don Gutierre *prescribes* death."[24] Gutierre's proclivity for metaphorical language is epitomized in the death threat he directs to Mencía:

> ¿No has visto ardiente llama
> perder la luz al aire que la hiere,
> y que a este tiempo de otra luz inflama
> la pavesa? Una vive y otra muere
> a sólo un soplo. Así desta manera
> la lengua de los vientos lisonjera

matarte la luz pudo,
y darme luz a mí.[25]

[Have you not seen a burning flame blown out
By a strong gust that at the same time kindles
A flame in a dull cinder? At one breath
A flame dies and another flame is born.
So, likewise, with one flick of its fawning
and flattering tongue the wind can, in one trice,
Deprive you of your flickering light and give
Some luster to myself.][26]

Gutierre states the obvious when he asks whether the wind that blows
out one flame may alternatively stoke another fire. Less obvious is his acknowledgment of Mencía's deceit, which consists of having extinguished a
candle to facilitate Enrique's escape from their home in the previous scene.
Gutierre does not directly confront Mencía on this lie, but speaks in the
enigmatic language of the Sphinx, whereby an incorrect answer results
in death. Gutierre does not *only* pose a question, nor does he *only* reveal
knowledge of Enrique's trespasses. More crucially, his elaborate metaphor
represents a veiled threat whereby the "wind's tongue" will not "extin-
guish" the light representing Mencía's life, but rather Gutierre will commit
the deed. It is revealing that he assigns the faculty of speech to the element
of air, qualifying it as flattering, hypocritical praise (*lisonjera*). Spoken with
a forked tongue, flattery employs language as a means of deception; the flat-
terer consciously assigns to the object a value that may be true or false, but
that does not accord with his or her own belief. Gutierre also speaks with
a forked tongue, because he acknowledges to himself that his final demonstrations of affection for Mencía are false. His underlying condemnation of
Mencía's deceit is therefore undermined by his own conscious obfuscation
of language.

Gutierre's tongue is not the only part of himself to be divided. In one of
the most extraordinary scenes in which Gutierre becomes entirely possessed
by jealousy, he acknowledges his own duplicity:

y así os receta y ordena
el médico de su honra
primeramente la dieta
del silencio, que es guardar
la boca, tener paciencia;
luego dice que apliquéis

a vuestra mujer finezas,
agrados, gustos, amores,
lisonjas, que son las fuerzas
defendibles, porque el mal
con el despego no crezca.[27]

[So this is what the Surgeon of his Honour
Prescribes for his sick patient. For your diet—
Silence; partake of it with your mouth closed:
And patience, too, take it in the same way.
Then to your wife apply kindnesses, favours,
Pleasures, endearments, flatteries, and caresses,
Since subterfuges are defensible
So that the sickness be not aggravated
By coldness or asperity—because
Jealousies, grievances, suspicions, threats
Instead of healing, make the sickness worse.][28]

In this passage Gutierre refers to himself in the third person, thus playing two roles: that of doctor and that of patient. His choice of metaphor is all the more ironic considering the schizophrenic nature of this "conversation." Furthermore, his split consciousness is not limited to a dual role. The general climate of repression Gutierre inhabits imposes silence as a means of maintaining social order and in turn leads him to internalize a repressive role. Like the figure of the *pharmakos*, "who has to be killed to strengthen," Gutierre represses and finally destroys a part of himself which gives voice to the ills assailing him.[29] This inquisitorial role is not limited to self-repression but extends to Mencía. His interrogation takes on a more "refined," sinister role, for in order to discover if she has, in fact, betrayed him, Gutierre adopts the language of seduction ("finezas, agrados, gustos, amores, lisonjas").

In *El médico* one of the most insidious and generalized forms of repression consists of self-censorship. Mencía is capable of speaking with great rhetorical intensity without ever once naming the person about whom she speaks.[30] Such omissions may even take place in the absence of an interlocutor, as is the case in the first act: apart from her former suitor, who lies unconscious, she is alone.[31] To name him necessarily implies recognizing and acknowledging his presence. As the drama unfolds, such an acknowledgment soon joins a newly created category of forbidden topics. According to this formula, a slip of the tongue becomes a fatal fall from grace. Repressing Enrique's name, however, does not eliminate his presence; on the contrary, his name gains considerably more significance than it might have had otherwise. When Mencía mistakes Gutierre's voice for that of Enrique, and warns him to stay away, the mere mention of his royal title becomes explosive. The dramatic impact, as well as Gutierre's shock, is considerable.

Mencía internalizes the mechanisms that prevent her from speaking to such a degree that she sacrifices the freedom to think in private—a sacrifice which Gutierre does not make. On the contrary, Gutierre externalizes his rage, although he is loath to say the word "jealousy" even in private: "¿Celos dije? / ¡Qué mal hice! Vuelva, vuelva / al pecho la voz" ("Jealousy," did I say? Then I spoke wrongly. / Come back, come back, my voice, into my breast!).[32] One of the most notable exceptions to this rule occurs when he can no longer repress his rage and says to Mencía:

> llegar pudiera
> a tener . . . ¿qué son celos?
> átomos, ilusiones y desvelos . . . ;
> no más que de una esclava, una criada
> por sombra imaginada,
> con hechos inhumanos,
> a pedazos sacara con mis manos
> el corazón, y luego
> envuelto en sangre, desatado en fuego,
> el corazón comiera
> a bocados, la sangre me bebiera,
> el alma le sacara
> y el alma, ¡Vive Dios!, despedazara,
> si capaz de dolor el alma fuera.[33]

> ["Jealous," you say?
> What do you know of jealousy? What is it?
> I have not got the least idea! But if
> I *had*— . . .
> —the slightest inkling—
> Or felt the slightest twinge—(But what it is
> I cannot guess)—or felt the least suspicious
> Even of a slave, or servant, I would fetch
> Her heart out of her body piece by piece
> With my bare hands, and spattered with her blood,
> And breathing fire, would wolf it raw, in lumps,
> Drinking the blood like wine! I would draw forth

> Her soul, by God! And grind it into atoms
> If by then it were capable of feeling!][34]

This passage stands in stark contrast to the scenes that precede and follow it, for its rage issues forth with an intensity that is commensurate only with the degree of repression Gutierre exercises on his voice. His refusal to acknowledge his jealousy causes it to grow exponentially until he is no longer in control of himself. The silence he has held in such high esteem is momentarily suspended, and he reveals a private persona unseen until this moment. In his violent metamorphosis he assumes an identity that he has sought so hard to avoid, that is, that of one those "maridos viles / que pierden a sus agravios / el miedo, cuando lo dicen" (base / Husbands who do not seem to dread affront / though courting it with the affronts they give).[35] The mere mention of the word "jealousy" in his initial question triggers a reaction explosive in its suddenness. Without warning, Gutierre loses the critical distance needed to examine the passion that possesses him so entirely. He does not only *say* what jealousy is; he becomes the very thing he describes—the embodiment of jealousy.

The verbal violence of Gutierre's outburst foreshadows the physical violence that concludes the drama. He initially claims that jealousy is nothing but a figment of the imagination, and the subjunctive mode in which he frames the above passage (*sacara, comiera, bebiera*) indicates a purely hypothetical response. The images Gutierre conjures suggest otherwise. Hypothetically, were he to be jealous he would be capable of dismembering and cannibalizing a servant or slave. Hypothetically too, he would attempt to inflict pain on anything or anyone capable of experiencing pain. Such hypotheses reveal his capacity to deliver cruel and unusual punishment. Gutierre's violent rhetoric evokes a discourse that named practices such as cannibalism as grounds for the subjugation of people seventeenth-century Europeans considered "barbaric."[36] Gutierre, however, is a fourteenth-century Christian Spaniard of noble standing; he hardly qualifies for membership to the class of the dispossessed. As one who speaks of cannibalism, Gutierre temporarily assumes a marginal rhetorical position, but only as a pretext to subjugate those who possess less authority than himself.

Throughout the drama, the protagonists' desire to alleviate their suffering through speech stands in contrast to their actual self-restraint. In Mencía's case, her extreme caution reveals a fear so great it prevents her from even naming the source of this fear.[37] Her private outbursts do not provide the cathartic effect for which she searches. On the contrary, speech becomes the very source of incrimination from the onset of the dramatic action:

> Mas ¿qué digo?
> ¿Qué es esto, cielos, qué es esto?
> Yo soy quien soy. Vuelva el aire
> los repetidos acentos
> que llevó; porque aun perdidos,
> no es bien que publiquen ellos
> lo que yo debo callar,
> porque ya, con más acuerdo,
> ni para sentir soy mía.[38]

> [But what is this I've said? I am myself.
> Then let the wind return my words, though lost
> In it, for it would not be well to publish
> What silence must conceal.][39]

Mencía abruptly interrupts her recollections of past romance by calling attention to her words ("¿qué digo?"). She second guesses herself, then makes a claim to selfhood ("yo soy quien soy") that is just as soon subverted by her self-estrangement ("ni para sentir soy mía").[40] Her monologue wavers between self-affirmation and self-doubt in a process that reveals the tortuous path of a modern consciousness in which the divided self takes on an increasingly significant role. She desires to speak without being heard and, having spoken, want to take back what she has said. But words once spoken are only retrieved with difficulty, if at all. The self's relationship to language becomes particularly problematic, for Mencía places demands on language that it cannot meet. The verb *publicar* is significant in this regard, for it calls attention to the permanence of words whereby the private becomes public. Like rumor, slander, or gossip, the "publication" of words may subject the author to unwarranted scrutiny.

Contrary to Mencía, Gutierre assigns a positive value to silence. For him, it serves as an effective antidote to the dangers of speech. Toward the end of the second act, as he stalks his own wife, he reveals the esteem in which he holds silence:

> En el mudo silencio
> de la noche, que adoro y reverencio
> por sombra aborrecida,
> como sepulcro de la humana vida,

de secreto he venido
hasta mi casa, sin haber querido
avisar a Mencía.[41]

[In the dead silence of the night
Which I with reverence adore,
The sepulchre of life and light
Whose shade all other men abhor,
I have returned in secret without telling
My wife of my acquittal by the King
So that she would be ignorant about
My coming here.][42]

Here Gutierre personifies silence as "mute," thus reiterating the importance of secrecy defined as another form of repressed speech. This secrecy has a subversive facet; incapable of repressing himself or others, he is compelled to behave surreptitiously. Secrecy does not guarantee him the anonymity, reputation, or honor he so desperately desires. On the contrary, it casts a deep shadow on what is presumed to constitute honorable behavior. Gutierre persists until the end of the drama to act in secret and to repress what he considers undesirable. He employs another to kill his wife by bleeding her to death, since by murdering her himself Gutierre necessarily incriminates himself not only as an assassin but also as a cuckold. Rather than risk this social shame, he prefers to implicate another in his crime—even to the point where he considers murdering his wife's murderer. Yet Mencía's dead body persists as an unmistakable sign not only of Gutierre's lost honor but also of his treachery. Mencía has the last "word" at the price of her life. That Gutierre is directly responsible for his wife's murder therefore represents an open secret. The secrecy that silence and darkness provide Gutierre is fleeting, although he regards it with adoration and reverence accorded divine worship. He actively seeks the dark shadows of the night from which others recoil precisely for its close association to the eternal sleep of death.

In *El médico* a constellation of characters support a general climate of repression. The most politically powerful of the protagonists is King Pedro.[43] As the embodiment of absolute power, he decides which of his subjects speak and when. The exchange between the monarch and the fool or *gracioso* embodies the extreme imbalance of power between them:

REY. ¿Quién sois?

COQUÍN. ¿Yo señor?

REY. Vos.

COQUÍN. Yo
(¡válgame el cielo!) Soy quien
vuestra Majestad quisiere,
sin quitar y sin poner,
porque un hombre muy discreto
me dio por consejo ayer,
no fuese quien en mi vida
vos no quisieseis; y fue
de manera la lición,
que antes, agora, y después,
quien vos quisiéredes sólo
fui, quien gustareis seré,
quien os place soy.[44]

[REY. Who are you?

COQUÍN. Who? Me,
My lord?

REY. You!

COQUÍN. I, may heaven help me, am
One whom your Majesty would like without
Subtraction or addition. A discreet
Person, but yesterday, advised me never
To be or practice what you would not like.
I took the lesson so much to my heart
That both before it, then, and afterwards
I've always been a man you would have liked,
And still I am, and always shall be too.][45]

In this exchange, Coquín transforms a banal question—"who are you?"—
into an extraordinary opportunity for reflection on the relationship between power and identity. If, as Coquín suggests, one's self is subject to the
King's absolute authority, then Coquín is not in a position to say who he
is. Even a proper name, one of the primordial signs of identity, is subject to
the external forces of the King's power. According to Coquín, the King's
authority is not even subject to the passage of time; Coquín was, is, and
will be forever subject to the King. As such, he suggests that the powerless
cannot claim an identity, since a degree of autonomy is necessary in order
to make self-determination possible. The underlying assumption is that a
redistribution of power is vital to such claims. Coquín adds that his view
are not unique, for he claims to have been cautioned by "un hombre muy

discreto," suggesting that common wisdom also advises great caution in matters of royal authority.

Coquín's reply to the King reveals the wit proper to a *gracioso*. He does not withhold his name every time it is asked, nor does he seize every opportunity to comment on the complex relations between power and identity. Rather, his long answer to the King's short question reveals a deep distrust and fear of power as well as a certain resistance to the King's demands. Fear compels Coquín to hide from the King, just as fear prompts Mencía to "engañar con la verdad" (to cheat / By telling him the truth).[46] Similarly, Coquín's submission to the King resembles Mencía's submission to her husband. Both conceal information by any means necessary in order to protect themselves from the violent exercise of power. The survival of both servant and wife depends on having a degree of control over what they say or, alternatively, keep silent.

Leonor, the character Gutierre weds after murdering Mencía, both contributes to and is a victim of the drama's repressive climate. In the past, Gutierre pursued Leonor, but abandons her on the suspicion of betrayal. Believing that she has been wronged by his seduction and subsequent abandonment, she directly seeks redress in the King's court:

> ¿Con qué razones, gran señor, herida
> la voz, diré a tanto amor postrada,
> aunque el desdén me publicó ofendida,
> la voluntad me confesó obligada?[47]

> [By what excuses can my wounded voice
> Explain, my lord, how to such love I yielded?
> And though I seemed to show disdain in public
> In secret I was gratified.][48]

Her choice of verbs (*publicar* and *confesar*) suggests two conflicting, but interrelated aspects of language. To publish is to literally make public, while confession suggests the sharing of words on a much smaller, often intimate scale. And yet, both publishing and confessing share a similar function by which words are repeated and therefore subject to change. What Leonor is willing to confess stands in contrast to the persona she projects in public ("el desdén me publicó ofendida, / la voluntad me confesó obligada"). This division of the self provokes an anxiety that is embodied by her difficulty in finding the right words to accuse Gutierre without herself being accused. Furthermore, Leonor assigns functions of speech to abstract concepts where are incapable of speech. By shifting the origin of speech from people to concepts such as disdain and free will, she distances herself from her own voice and by extension from her own actions. Her strategy becomes one of incrimination by means of insinuation in which the mere mention of the crime casts doubt on the subject.

Leonor's interlocutor is the King, and the success of her request depends on her power of persuasion. In her encomium to the King, she ascribes to him divine powers of destruction:

> Júpiter español, cuya cuchilla
> rayos esgrime el templado acero,
> cuando blandida al aire alumbra y brilla;
> sangriento giro, que entre nubes de oro,
> corta los cuellos de uno y otro moro.[49]

> [As the great Jupiter of Spain,
> From whose bright sword of tempered steel
> Flash thunderbolts and showers of fire
> When flourished in a crimson gyre
> Between the golden clouds, it floors
> The ranks and squadrons of the Moors.][50]

Violence in its most destructive manifestation is posited as a positive value in this exercise of *captatio benevolentiae*. The image of the Moors' slashed throats is rendered all the more violent as it is framed by the contrasting images of light and gold. Although the representation of the Christian warrior with raised sword over the infidel was a conventional image in seventeenth-century Spain, it is not insignificant that Leonor equates the King from Castile with Jupiter, a pagan god of war. Here, she emphasizes the King's military prowess, not his Christianity and as such reinforces the violent undercurrent traversing her plea for revenge. To demand such revenge, as Leonor does, or to take revenge into one's own hands, as does Gutierre at the conclusion of the play, "can be seen as the sacrifice of innocent blood, a perverse atonement for the imperfections of humanity."[51] Leonor's petition also reminds us of the hierarchical order of the play, where value is assigned according to one's place in society. Moors are violently subordinated to Christians, even when the latter's behavior calls into question the very values on which Christianity is presumably based.

In *El médico*, problematic couples such as monarch and subject, husband and wife, master and slave belong to a complex web of relations in which the political and personal are inextricably bound. Gutierre's discourse, for example, takes on a political dimension when demonstrating affection for Mencía early in the drama:

> Yo sin alma en la prisión
> por estar en ti, mi bien
> darme libertad fue bien,
> para que en esta ocasión
> alma y vida con razón
> otra vez se viese unida;
> porque estaba dividida,
> teniendo en prolija calma,
> en una prisión el alma
> y en otra prisión la vida.[52]

> [I lived
> Without my soul in prison, my beloved,
> Since it was here in you. To grant this brief
> Liberty, was to join my soul and body,
> For they were both divided until now
> Wearing out listless hours in separate cells—
> The one imprisoned there, the other here.][53]

Gutierre's "prison" takes on an ambivalent meaning. In one sense, it constitutes the physical space in which the state stands as an official instrument of punishment. But according to Gutierre, the prison also refers to his wife, as he is not free without her as she holds an essential part of his divided self. Gutierre's observations reflect the official conception by which a married couple is indivisible until death do them part. The displacement of the personal into the realm of the political also suggests that Gutierre submits voluntarily to the power of the state; that is, he consents to the restrictions that are imposed on him. This displacement becomes particularly problematic at the moment Gutierre suspects his wife of adultery. If the conjugal bond may only be undone at the price of Mencía's life, one may ask at what price the bond between subject and state may also be undone.

In a critical moment near the conclusion of the drama, Mencía writes a letter to her former suitor. Believing Enrique's sudden departure from Seville might incriminate her, she persuades him to stay. When she commits words to paper, she crosses the line separating her from the public world for the first time; she reaches beyond the confines of an increasingly asphyxiating private space. She assumes language will speak on her behalf; instead she inadvertently writes her own death sentence. For Gutierre, her letter represents the visible evidence of her infidelity; but more is at stake here, for his rage needs little reason to kill. In fact, he has already passed his death sentence on Mencía.[54] Why is it then at this particular moment that he decides to take action? His response to Mencía is revealing, for he writes it on the same paper as Mencía's letter to Enrique: "El amor te adora, el honor te aborrece; y así el uno te mata, y el otro te avisa: dos horas tienes de vida; cristiana eres, salva el alma, que la vida es imposible" ("Though Love adores you, Honour must abhor you. Though Honour slays you, Love would give you warning and counsel. You have two more hours of life. You are a Christian: save your soul, since, now, it is impossible to save your life").[55] His warning represents a symbolic gesture of his final authority over his wife, since it establishes a verbal barrier preventing her words from going anywhere beyond the confines of their property. The prose in which he writes stands in stark contrast to the rest of the verse in which the drama is written and suggests his ability to impose his authority over all matters linguistic or otherwise. In other words, Mencía is no match for Gutierre's verbal or physical dueling. He is in a position to match words to their actions—language is still on his side while Mencía remains language's victim.

The idea to write to Enrique does not belong to Mencía, but rather to her slave who plays a more significant role than critics have generally acknowledged. An exception to this rule is D. W. Cruickshank's note on the role of the "esclava herrada," which Calderón assigns to Jacinta:

> Herrada, sin duda con una S y un clavo (es-clavo), como dice Pedro Crespo en *El alcalde de Zalamea*. Según Covarrubias, 'pocas vezes, o nunca se hierran los esclavos, salvo quando son fugitivos e incorregibles: y si no son Cristianos no tiene tanto inconveniente.'[56]

> [She was no doubt branded with the letter S and the figure of a nail, as Pedro Crespo states in *El alcalde de Zalamea*. According to Covarrubias, "slaves are rarely or never branded, except when they are fugitives or incorrigible: and if they are not Christians it is not so inconvenient to brand them."]

By this definition Jacinta represents the dimmest star in the constellation of power relations in *El médico*. She literally carries the burden of language on her body for the sign of slavery is cruelly branded on her face. Covarrubias's definition suggests that such a mark did not weigh heavily on the conscience of the slaves' masters, since heretics were not considered deserving of the same treatment as believers. Calderón does not name Jacinta's religious affiliation, and in the frontispiece of the princeps edition, her role is generically assigned as "una esclava" (a slave). However, given the setting of *El médico* in fourteenth-century Seville, it is not incongruous to identify Jacinta as non-Christian. As such, she would represent a source of fear, reviled as both a powerful and potentially corrupting and corruptible force. Such a characterization is supported by the text. Jacinta betrays the trust Mencía places in her by facilitating the Infante's entry into their garden. But it is not insignificant that such a trust is betrayed at the price of the slave's freedom. At the beginning of the second act, Enrique makes Jacinta an offer that is difficult to refuse:

> Si la libertad, Jacinta,
> que te prometí, presumes
> poco premio a bien tan grande,
> pide más, y no te excuses
> por cortedad: vida y alma
> es bien que por tuyas juzgues.[57]

> [The liberty I promised you, Jacinta,
> Is nothing to what I shall give you more
> If you so much as ask it. Heart and soul
> You've put me in your debt for evermore.][58]

Jacinta accepts Enrique's offer and as such, the slave's behavior conforms to a literary commonplace at least as old as *La Celestina* whereby servants betray their masters for material gain. What is more unusual is what Enrique offers in exchange for free entry into Mencía's home: "vida y alma / es bien que por tuyas juzgues," literally, his life and soul. Despite his ulterior motives, Enrique's observation calls into question the legitimacy of Jacinta's bondage. As a slave, she is bound to her masters by force, not by virtue of her free will. The fact that she acquiesces to Enrique's proposition not only confirms her treachery but more importantly reflects her rejection of a social system that subordinates one person to another by force. As a slave, Jacinta is bound by the letter of the law to serve her masters, and her entire existence is bound by the words that constitute this law. Is it not possible, therefore, that one who is bound by words might just as well search for release by means of the word? In fact, it is she who urges her mistress to write the final, fatal letter to Enrique.

If speech promises to do political or personal justice to suffering by alleviating pain, *El medico* does not offer such relief. Rather, repression impairs the

possibility of expressions until actions replace words as a means of transforming reality. This transformation consists of the progressive destruction of that
reality. When Gutierre can no longer "signify" his pain, he takes recourse to
violence where objects of destruction are permitted to speak for themselves.
Such is the case when he presents the King with the Infante's dagger: "Y para
esto hable un testigo: / esta daga, esta brillante / lengua de acero elegante"
(let this dagger speak / With its fine, white, effulgent tongue of steel).[59]
Despite the dagger's brilliant "tongue," it communicates its message ambigu-
ously. Gutierre shows the dagger to the King as proof of the Infante's trespass,
but its appearance has quite the opposite effect on the King, who reads it as
a threat to his brother's life. As such, Gutierre does not speak for himself,
but transforms an inanimate object into a "witness" of a crime whose name
is incapable or unwilling of saying.

Later, Gutierre will transform a surgeon's scalpel into the crime weapon
itself. Words fail Gutierre, and he in turn fails to use language constructively.
Rather, he will use the surgeon's scalpel to write his frustration in Mencía's
blood. Ludovico, the surgeon who actually performs the deed, leaves his
bloody handprints as a trail pointing the way to Mencía's dead body. In his
statement to the King he confesses,

> Fui por las paredes
> como que quise arrimarme,
> manchando todas las puertas,
> por si pueden las señales
> descubrir la casa.[60]

> [my hands being covered with her blood,
> I, feigning to support myself against
> The Doors, kept daubing them with crimson hand-prints
> So to mark the house for recognition.][61]

The King "reads" this gruesome trail of blood, which will end in the
hand-print left on the door of the couple's home. Gutierre refers to his
final handprint as a metaphorical coat of arms that serves as an emblem
of his honor: "así pongo / mi mano en sangre bañada / a la puerta; que
el honor / con sangre, señor, se lava" (I who deal in Honour / So place
a bloodstained hand upon my door / For Honour can be only washed in
blood).[62] With these words, Calderón calls into question the nobility that
a coat of arms is presumed to represent. If, in fact, this nobility is based
on the shedding of innocent blood, and not only on the blood inherited
from one's ancestors, then *El médico* shines a critical light on power as it

is exercised not only by a husband, but also by a nobleman, or the King himself. It is not irrelevant that the King should qualify Gutierre's crime in these terms: "*cuerdamente / sus agravios satisfizo*" (cautiously he settled his effront).[63] This also represents a politically expedient response, since Gutierre's crime saves the King from having to assume responsibility for his brother's adulterous trespasses against one of his subjects. The King thus conveniently keeps affairs of the heart separate from affairs of the State. Whether such a separation is possible or ethical remains open to question, given that the King is fully cognizant of the victim's innocence. In fact, the King reasserts his authority over both personal and political matters by uniting Leonor and Gutierre in marriage over the latter's objections. The marriage that concludes *El médico* represents more than a joyless match; it suggests the overall failure of the protagonists to draw any kind of meaning from the sequence of events leading to the final tragedy of Mencía's death. Just as significantly, it suggests the limits of the conjugal bond to unite its members in any effective manner when marriage is not contracted of one's free will.

Notes

1. Umberto Eco argues that performers necessarily function as signs. A man who represents another man "is no more a world object among world objects—he has become a semiotic device; he is now a *sign*." Eco, "Semiotics of Theatrical Performance," 110. This approach to drama also raises the question of what kind of "sign" a married woman might represent the moment she appears on the seventeenth-century Spanish stage. The full-length plays suggest that her appearance at the onset of the action represents a sign of impending doom that is in no way resolved, but rather ends in tragedy. In contrast, the short interludes such as Cervantes's *entremeses* examined in the previous chapter, the wife's initial appearance practically guarantees a comic outcome.

2. Saffar, "Anxiety of Identity: Gutierre's Case in *El médico de su honra*," 110.

3. Bennassar, *Los españoles*, 194. Bruce W. Wardropper's comments on the subject of honor are particularly relevant as they focus on the connection between honor and marriage: "The *drama de honor* . . . presents married couples; conjugal honor has largely replaced possessive love as the dominating motive; jealousy, *celos de honor*, is either admirable or base, but never silly. This, as Cervantes has pointed out, is because marriage involves a sacramental relationship, therefore, where honor is threatened God is interested." Wardropper, "Poetry and Drama in Calderón's *El médico de su honra*," 7.

4. For a summary of these views see Cruickshank, *Calderón de la Barca, El médico de su honra*.

5. González Echevarría, *Celestina's Brood*, 87.

6. Calderón de la Barca, *El médico de su honra*, lines 2079–80.

7. Ibid., lines 2131–34.

8. Calderón de la Barca, *The Surgeon of His Honour*, 58.

9. Calderón de la Barca, *El médico de su honra*, lines 550–53. Calderón de la Barca, *The Surgeon of His Honour*, 16.

10. Calderón de la Barca, *El médico de su honra*, lines 1585–92.

11. Calderón de la Barca, *The Surgeon of His Honour*, 44.

12. Alexander A. Parker observes the difference between Gutierre and Mencía when each of them attempts to avert conflict: "The two methods of curing oneself should be noted. Mencía does it by shouting, Guiterre by keeping quiet; while his way is not prudent, it would be so if the specter of jealousy did not come between Gutierre and his reason. To think that jealousy could have a basis transforms him from a rational man into passionate fury." Parker, "Los amores y noviazgos clandestinos en el mundo dramático-social de Calderón," 148. In either case, they both precipitate catastrophe.

13. Calderón de la Barca, *El médico de su honra*, lines 122–31.

14. Calderón de la Barca, *The Surgeon of His Honour*, 7.

15. Aurora Egido's observations regarding *La vida es sueño* are equally applicable to Mencía's soliloquy: "The will to speak and write appears as a painful process, akin to crying, but unavoidable when the poet desires to make his case public and to break the silence." Egido, "La vida es sueño y los idiomas del silencio," 97. Daniel Rogers provides a systematic examination of the many references to silence in "'Tienen los celos pasos de ladrones': Silence in Calderón's *El médico de su honra*." The tension produced by speech and silence also plays a prominent role in Calderón's *No hay cosa como callar*; *Psalle et Sile*; *La fiera, el rayo y la piedra*; and *Eco y Narciso*.

16. Walter Benjamin alludes to this sense of loss in Calderón's works: "The word 'history' stands written on the countenance of nature in the characters of transience. The allegorical physiognomy of nature-history, which is put on stage . . . is present in reality in the form of the ruin." Benjamin, *The Origin of German Tragic Drama*, 177. In effect, space and time produce an intense sense of anguish in Mencía's speech from which she cannot escape.

17. Calderón de la Barca, *El médico de su honra*, lines 565–74.

18. Calderón de la Barca, *The Surgeon of His Honour*, 17.

19. Mary Gaylord observes that "marriage in the *comedia* frequently acts as a moment that the action simultaneously desires and avoids, because it is precisely the moment that denies the dramatic game. The dramas of revenge, in contrast, make possession its primary, fatal premise. By following the love-honor itinerary through the mirror, Calderón demystifies marriage as a symbol of harmony, but he does not take away its gravity. Within marriage, honor possesses absolute seriousness, not because a crude exterior code demands it, but because now a dance of self-definition that the man and woman dance incessantly with each other is performed." Gaylord, "Amor y honor a traves del espejo," 873–74. Mencía's reflection on her past reflects

this "fatal premise"; her present spirals downward as a result of it, revealing the imperfections of an externally imposed conjugal promise.

20. Jonathan Culler comments on the communicative strengths of figurative language with particular emphasis on metaphor: "Whatever may be true of other figures, metaphors generally make claims that could in principle be restated as propositions, albeit with difficulty and prolixity. Doubtless for this reason, metaphor has long been thought of as the figure *par excellence* through which the writer can display creativity and authenticity: his metaphors are read as artistic inventions grounded in perceptions of relations in the world. Culler, *The Pursuit of Signs*, 191. Similarly, the protagonists will recur to metaphor as a means of communicating subjects they consider unspeakable.

21. Calderón de la Barca, *El médico de su honra*, lines 240–42.

22. Ruiz Ramón, *Calderón nuestro contemporáneo*, 54.

23. Calderón de la Barca, *El médico de su honra*, lines 202–5. Calderón de la Barca, *The Surgeon of His Honour*, 9.

24. Wardropper, "Poetry and Drama in Calderón's El médico de su honra," 4.

25. Calderón de la Barca, *El médico de su honra*, lines 2003–9.

26. Calderón de la Barca, *The Surgeon of His Honour*, 55.

27. Calderón de la Barca, *El médico de su honra*, lines 1672–82.

28. Calderón de la Barca, *The Surgeon of His Honour*, 46.

29. Frye, *Anatomy of Criticism: Four Essays*, 148.

30. Alberto Castilla comments on how the characters' lack of communication leads to devastating results: "The characters in *El médico de su honra* are hermetic beings, closed, self-contained. They rarely speak directly, and they always try to resolve their problems by recurring to the king . . . the lack of communication as an existential conflict appears at all levels between the characters . . . and they are the source of the solitude and disenchantment that pervade the mood of the drama. Man is unable to communicate with anyone, except himself." Castilla, "El arte teatral de Calderón en El médico de su honra," 406.

31. Isaac Benabu writes that "there are many soliloquies that highlight the characters' isolation. When two characters address one another, what the spectator presences is less an act of communication than one that attempts to circumvent free expression." Benabu, "Who Is the Protagonist?," 20.

32. Calderón de la Barca, *El médico de su honra*, lines 1697–99. Calderón de la Barca, *The Surgeon of His Honour*, 46.

33. Calderón de la Barca, *El médico de su honra*, lines 2019–31.

34. Calderón de la Barca, *The Surgeon of His Honour*, 55–56.

35. Calderón de la Barca, *El médico de su honra*, lines 2156–58.

36. Take, for example, Juan Ginés de Sepúlveda's *A Treatise on the Just Causes of the War against the Indians*: "what temperance or what gentleness can you expect from men who were given over to every sort of intemperance and abominable lewdness and who used to eat human flesh? . . . They were engaged continually and ferociously in war with each other, which they waged with such rage that victory was worthless

if they could not satisfy their monstrous hunger with the flesh of their enemies." Sepúlveda concludes that "God has given great and very clear signs with respect to the extermination of these barbarians." Sepúlveda, *Tratado sobre las justas causas de la guerra contra los indios*, 228–30.

37. Francisco Ruiz Ramón distinguishes Mencía's fear from that of her counterparts in other honor plays: "In contrast to Leonor [*A secreto agravio, secreta venganza*], Mencía must defend herself from the sexual aggression of the *Infante*. . . . Her last words, "Why don't the beasts help me?" significantly, and with a cruel irony that has curiously gone unnoticed by the critics, connect with Gutierre's voice and his imminent entrance in this scene. Mencía's growing fear throughout the act and the entire action responds to his voice, and with her words, she seems to reaffirm the Gutierre/ beast association. . . . It involves, however, an ambiguous dramatic clarity, given that it posits guilt as the consequence of fear, and fear is going to be the great force that completely possesses Mencía. Ruiz Ramón, *Calderón nuestro contemporáneo*, 64.

38. Calderón de la Barca, *El médico de su honra*, lines 131–39.

39. Calderón de la Barca, *The Surgeon of His Honour*, 7.

40. Leo Spitzer's study of the expression "soy quien soy" does not refer to Mencía's invocation of the same phrase; nevertheless, it sheds light on the role the past plays in affirming the self: "The noble who *is who he is* does not define himself with any absolute, precise trait; *he is what he should be*, given his particular traditions. He is modest within his haughtiness, as if to say 'Perhaps I cannot justify being who I am thanks to my ancestry, but I am *everything* my past has made me.' He seems to accept life's vagaries but at the same time affirms the existence of a mold that his own lineage has created." Spitzer, "Soy quien soy," 125. Mencía, in similar fashion, asserts her right to claim her past and the role the past has played in determining her identity.

41. Calderón de la Barca, *El médico de su honra*, lines 1862–66.

42. Calderón de la Barca, *The Surgeon of His Honour*, 50.

43. Fox, "The Literary Use of History: *El médico de su honra* in Contexts," 70–80.

44. Calderón de la Barca, *El médico de su honra*, lines 711–23.

45. Calderón de la Barca, *The Surgeon of His Honour*, 21–22.

46. Calderón de la Barca, *El médico de su honra*, line 1354.

47. Ibid., lines 633–36.

48. Calderón de la Barca, *The Surgeon of His Honour*, 19.

49. Calderón de la Barca, *El médico de su honra*, lines 612–16.

50. Calderón de la Barca, *The Surgeon of His Honour*, 19.

51. Dunn, "Honour and the Christian Background in Calderón," 83.

52. Calderón de la Barca, *El médico de su honra*, lines 1201–10.

53. Calderón de la Barca, *The Surgeon of His Honour*, 34.

54. Immediately after hearing the exchange between the King and Enrique that reveals the latter's betrayal, Gutierre says, "cuando llega / un marido a saber que hay / celos, faltará la ciencia; / y es la cura postrera / que el médico de honor hacer intenta." Calderón de la Barca, *El médico de su honra*, lines 1708–12.

55. Ibid., line 2496.

56. Ibid., note 44.

57. Ibid., lines 1029–34.

58. Calderón de la Barca, *The Surgeon of His Honour*, 30.

59. Calderón de la Barca, *El médico de su honra*, lines 2103–108. Calderón de la Barca, *The Surgeon of His Honour*, 59.

60. Calderón de la Barca, *El médico de su honra*, lines 2700–705.

61. Calderón de la Barca, *The Surgeon of His Honour*, 75–76.

62. Calderón de la Barca, *El médico de su honra*, lines 2936–38. Calderón de la Barca, *The Surgeon of His Honour*, 82.

63. Ibid., lines 2792–93. Calderón de la Barca, *The Surgeon of His Honour*, 78.

CHAPTER FIVE

Marriage's End in Widowhood in Lope de Vega's *La viuda valenciana*

[A]ndando más los tiempos y creciendo más la malicia, se instituyó la orden de los caballeros andantes, para defender doncellas, amparar las viudas y socorrer a los huérfanos y a los menesterosos.

—Miguel de Cervantes Saavedra, *El ingenioso don Quijote de la Mancha*

Las tocas negras y los pensamientos verdes.

—Gonzalo Correas

Widows represent some of the most commonplace yet controversial characters from as early as Juan Ruiz's *El libro de buen amor* (1330[?]). Sebastián de Covarrubias's *Tesoro de la lengua castellana o española* (1611) suggests the importance Spanish society assigns widows in the early modern period by providing a definition for the feminine *biuda* while altogether overlooking the *biudo* or widower.[1] In societies that define women in terms of their relationship to men, as is the case in early modern Spain, widowhood often represents one of the most devastating events in a woman's life in that it "carried immense social, economic, and psychological consequences for a woman."[2] A number of contradictions riddle the figure of the widow in the *comedia* in light of the conduct manuals dictating her behavior. While these manuals portray widows as hapless victims of their husband's death, more often than not, the *comedia* and other literary works of the period celebrate widows as women in possession of considerable wealth and beauty. The representation of widows is compelling because it provides insight into an anomalous female figure given her freedom from spousal authority. Writers during this period tend to portray widows as women who possess privileged information regarding sex, and such knowledge may either enhance or put into peril a widow's social status. In either case, there is an underlying assumption that her conjugal experience represents powerful currency in the fluctuating economy of social relations.

While it may appear obvious to the modern reader that death represents an end to the conjugal bond, during the early modern period, not all authors agree that this is, in fact, the case. For example, Erasmus's *In Praise of Marriage* (also titled *An Example of a Letter of Persuasion*) suggests that the bonds of matrimony may actually extend beyond the grave: "But death alone dissolves wedlock, if indeed it does dissolve it. It is only dissolved in the case of those who seek another marriage. As long as wedded love persists, the marriage is not considered to be dissolved."[3] While it is possible that Erasmus makes this claim for rhetorical purposes, it underscores the growing attention authors devote to the figure of the widow in the early modern period.[4] Perhaps what is most significant in these comments is the value they assign to "wedded love." That such a sentiment might actually *transcend* death represents a persuasive argument in favor of the institution of marriage. However, the fact that Erasmus and other moralists value marriage most at the moment of death is an irony that is not lost to writers in early modern Spain. Particularly in a dramatic work such as Lope de Vega's *La viuda valenciana* (1620) there exists an underlying sense that, for many a widow, death not only represents the end of marriage, but also an *end* to which she aspired while her husband was alive. Her husband's death releases her from her conjugal duties and in turn affords her a previously unknown freedom. Such a sentiment stands in stark contrast to the moral treatises devoted to regulating widows' behavior in the strictest terms possible.

The appearance of the widow in Spanish literary works—an independent woman by the standards of the period—has begun to attract increasing critical attention.[5] The many intriguing contradictions riddling this figure in prescriptive as well as literary texts in early modern Spain may account for this attention.[6] On the one hand, the widow drawn from the biblical tradition suffers the consequences of death's devastation. Left to fend for herself, she is vulnerable to poverty, sickness, and death. As early as the twelfth century, canon law regards widows and orphans as *miserabiles personae*, "a label that corresponds closely to the modern term *disadvantaged persons*."[7] Taking Fernando de Rojas's *La Celestina* as a point of departure, where the protagonist of the title claims that "[a]sí que donde no hay varón, todo bien fallece," (wherever a man is missing, all good things die), Marjorie Ratcliffe's study characterizes widows during the Middle Ages as "pobres y solas, sin el respaldo económico de un marido ni la compañía de hijos que la cuidaran" (poor and solitary, without the economic support of a husband nor the company of children who might care for her).[8]

In contrast to the figure of the downtrodden widow, Spanish writers in the early modern period often represent them as possessing great physical youth and beauty as well as substantial economic resources. Both Cervantes's contemporaries as well as his predecessors choose to portray these self-sufficient widows over their disadvantaged counterparts. It is for this reason too, that Don Quixote's claim to support widows cited at the beginning of this chapter echoes a commonplace as well as an irony. By the time he decides to take up knighthood, a number of noteworthy and often well-to-do widows had replaced their subaltern counterparts, at least in literary discourses. Don Quixote's defense of widows as *miserablis personae* in imitation of his most cherished literary heroes is thus redundant in practice, if noble in intent.[9]

Seminal works such as *El libro de buen amor* suggest the degree to which Don Quixote's characterization of widows is anachronistic considering the number of wealthy widows that abound in both literary and historical discourses as early as the fourteenth century. To cite one example, in *El libro de buen amor* don Melón summarizes the widow doña Endrina's seductive qualities:

> De talla muy apuesta, de gestos amorosa,
> doñeguil, muy loçana, placentera e fermosa,
> cortés e mesurada, falaguera, donosa,
> graçiosa e risueña, amor en toda cosa.
> La más noble figura de quantas yo ver pud,
> biuda, rica es mucho e moça de juventud,
> e bien acostumbrada; es de Calataút:
> de mí era vezina, mi muerte e mi salut.[10]

> [Her wanton form was eloquent, her glances were inflaming
> For she was jaunty, graceful, gay, and lief for lovers' gaming,
> Yet coy resides, with modesty her ardent nature taming,
> Although her eyes passionate—love's one desire proclaiming.
> The noblest figure she possessed that ever I have known;
> A widow rich she was yet scarce beyond her girlhood grown.
> Above the dames of Calatud she stood as on a throne;
> My neighbor too, my life and death, for whom I lived alone.][11]

Here Doña Endrina's status as a widow does not isolate her socially; rather, widowhood represents one of her many attributes including wealth, beauty, and experience. By stating that she is *bien acostumbrada*, Don Melón glosses over what exactly constitutes an experience he characterizes in positive terms. However, as a widow who demonstrates *amor en toda cosa*, she is likely to have expertise in all matters conjugal, and if this is the case, such an endorsement of sexual knowledge over ignorance is noteworthy in a work written by a cleric. Through the voice of don Melón, Juan Ruiz suggests that a widow's experience in matters of sexual seduction may be more desirable than the qualities conventionally associated with virginity. While a girl of marriageable age might possess the same qualities as Doña Endrina, in the eyes of the moralists it is her virginity that makes her especially desirable. In this regard, it is remarkable *El libro de buen amor* should deviate so far from the treatises that exalt virginity as a woman's most precious currency in the marriage market.

Doña Endrina's sexual experience and economic independence distinguish her from the "disadvantaged persons" Don Quixote lumps together in one category along with virgins and orphans. Much of the cultural anxiety surrounding widows may, in fact, be due to what Marjo Buitelaar describes as their "potentially unfettered sexual longing."[12] This longing, as well as the anxiety it produces, is evident in early modern Spanish letters. Juan Luis Vives's *The Education of the Christian Woman*, for example, characterizes widows' sexuality as a disruptive force that must be constrained at all costs. Extolling qualities such as frugality, religious devotion, and above all, chastity, *The Education* demands that widows obey a code of behavior governing the most intimate aspects of their lives. The moral views that *The Education* preaches therefore stand in direct contradiction to the inherent ambiguity of *El libro de buen amor*. This morality is at even further odds from works such as Lope de Vega's *La viuda valenciana* as we will later see in this discussion.

A cursory glance at the section headings of the third and final part of Vives's *Instrucción* titled "On Widows" reveals the degree of control the narrator expects them to exercise over their actions at the moment of their husband's death:

1. Del luto o llanto de las viudas
2. Del enterramiento del marido
3. De la memoria que ha de tener del marido
4. De la continencia y honestidad de la viuda
5. De qué manera se ha de haber en casa

    6. De qué manera se habrá fuera de casa
    7. De las segundas bodas[13]

    [1. On the Mourning of Widows
    2. On the Husband's Funeral
    3. On the Memory of One's Husband
    4. On the Chastity and Moral Rectitude of a Widow
    5. How They Should Conduct Themselves at Home
    6. How She Should Behave in Public
    7. On Second Marriages][14]

As these headings make abundantly clear, few actions on the part of a widow escape the narrator's attention. From a widow's display of emotion—she should not cry too much or too little—to the very texture of the clothes she wears, *The Education* inscribes widows within narrow social bounds. From the onset, the narrator goes to considerable lengths to explain why a husband's death represents *the* most catastrophic event in a woman's life: "La buena mujer, muerto su marido, sepa haber recibido el mayor daño y perdimiento que venir le podía . . . perecido no sólo la mitad de su ánima . . . mas aun toda ella haber sido quitada a sí misma, y de todo en todo muerta y acabada" (The holy woman should know that when her husband has died, she has suffered a most grievous loss . . . not only has half her soul perished . . . but her whole self has been wrested from her and annihilated).[15] This statement unambiguously presupposes a woman's loss of identity upon her husband's death; at the moment a woman is widowed, she is socially dead and finished according to *The Education.* The insistence on dictating widows' behavior in spite of its own claim that they have been reduced to social nonentities constitutes a recurring contradiction throughout the text.

Considering the publication success of *The Education,* it is possible that widows in early modern Spain were subject and ascribed to its rules. Still, the minute and vivid descriptions of what widows are *not* supposed to do suggest a very different social reality. The narrator repeatedly admonishes women, who rather than mourn their husband's death, indulge in their newfound freedom. For example, in the chapter titled "De qué manera se habrá fuera de casa" (How She Should Behave in Public) the narrator directs widows to refrain from any and all activities associated with worldly pleasure:

> es necesario que se dejen de toda manera de afeites y galas y vanidades, ni menos se curen de ir a los baños, ni a los convites y bailes, ni de oír músicas, ni de ver torneos ni juegos o fiestas, ni de ir por jardines en compañía de otras mujeres, ni mucho menos de hombres.[16]

[it is necessary to abandon all manner of makeup, formal attire, and vanities, and they should worry even less about going to the baths, feasts or dances, nor should they listen to music, see tournaments, games, parties, or go to parks in the company of other women, much less other men.]

Rather than participate in any semblance of public life, the narrator insists that widows lead the most private existence possible. Only religious and domestic spaces are deemed appropriate for widows, and even these are not above suspicion for *The Education* warns that she must take care not to talk too much with priests under the guise of devotion.[17] The specificity with which this passage refers to places that are off-limits to widows suggests that they might have, in fact, frequented them. Recent research suggests that widows participated in all manner of social and economic activities in spite of the moralists' admonitions.[18]

Still, the scope of the restrictions *The Education* places on widows is remarkable, for it not only excludes them from the public realm, but also isolates them within their own homes. One of the most striking instances occurs when the narrator advises widows to relinquish the care of their children to a "serious man," claiming that a mother's love for her children might prove overly indulgent. It further holds such mothers in disdain by claiming that society as a whole assumes ill-behaved children are the result of a widow's care: "Cada día vemos y es casi refrán común, que viendo al hijo de la viuda algo desobediente o desmandado, luego le dicen "criado de viuda" (We often see it happen that those brought up by a widow are less obedient. . . . Thus, the expression "a widow's child" has become a proverb among many peoples).[19] The reference to proverbial knowledge suggests the degree to which such attitudes prevailed at the time of *The Education*'s publication. In order to ensure a widow's full compliance with the rules it proposes, *The Education* also encourages her to live with her in-laws and her husband's relatives because, "es más riguroso el vivir con los parientes del marido que no con los propios, porque allí el amor suele ser menor y, por consiguiente, no hay tanto regalo, de donde nace la licencia del mal vivir" (respect for chastity is considered to be more severe among the relatives of the spouse than among the immediate family, since love is less strong there, and hence tolerance is almost nonexistent and freedom more restricted).[20] By this definition, love in nearly all of its manifestations including maternal or familial is tainted. Moreover, these restrictions virtually deny widows any kind of freedom, and just as critically, any affection for or from her next-of-kin. These rules of conduct presuppose that a widow's sexual experience represents a threat to social stability. The unstated assumption is that widows share a knowledge that is held first and foremost by men. To possess such knowledge necessarily implies sharing in the power that such knowledge makes possible in the first place. According to *The Education*, a widow possesses honor only when she has relinquished any and all agency in both public and private spheres.

In Vives's zeal to dictate a widow's behavior, he reveals women who are no longer subject to their husband's authority and who, in turn, subvert the ideal he holds in utmost respect: "hay algunas que se alegran de verse libres del marido, como si hubieran sacudido de sus cervices un muy grave yugo de servidumbre, o unas muy duras cadenas de cautiverio" (There are some women who rejoice at their husband's death as if they had shaken off some cruel yoke, as if liberated from the fetters of a despot, almost exulting in a newfound freedom).[21] While Vives is predictably critical of such merry widows—he claims they do not even deserve to be called "women"—his metaphors of marriage suggest the degree of control to which wives were subject during this period.[22] The "cruel yoke" as well as the "fetters of a despot" suggest metaphors of marriage that may, in fact, epitomize a moment in the history of marriage when most unions were arranged affairs and had little, if anything, to do with a couple's mutual affection. Works such as Calderón's *El médico de su honra*, examined in the previous chapter, affirm this dark side of marital relations. Considering a wife's subjection to her husband in early modern Spain, it is no wonder that she was eager to pay the price of admission to the *corral de comedias* where she could witness widows' defiance to the strictures prescribed in the didactic literature. Notwithstanding the specific restrictions *The Education* places on widows' freedom of movement—it even suggests that they walk and talk with decorum—they might not have led quite the cloistered life Vives advocates.

Contrary to the devout widow who leads a life of self-sacrifice, there exists another kind of widow who eschews social convention in favor of sexual expression. The narrator directly addresses just such a widow in this lengthy but vivid diatribe:

La vestidura vil y negra que traes es indicio de persona callada y honesta; pero si ella va galana y bien estirada y sin ruga alguna, y si tú la vas arrastrando por el suelo por parecer mayor que no eres, si adrede traes descosida o abierta la ropa por mostrar alguna parte agradable a los ojos de los miradores, si tu traes los zapaticos justos, lisos y muy polidos, y los chapines que con su crujir parece que andan llamando a cada paso a los que te ven, si traes los pechos muy apretados y fajados para que hinchen y resurtan hacia arriba y parezcan más redondos y rollizos, si tú traes los cabellos derramados por las espaldas, y las mechas caídas por las sienes y pechos, y si alguna vez dejas adrede caérsete el manto de los hombros por mostrar el pescuezo albo y las espaldas, y súbitamente, casi mostrando que te duele haber sido vista, te tornas muy presurosa a cubrir, si cuando por la calle haces como te cubres de vergüenza la cara y después te andas adesora descubriendo y de rato en rato mostrando aquello que a ti parece que más agrada a los ojos deshonestos, si éstas y otras cosas tales más a mujeres públicas, ¿parécete, por ventura, que haces bien?[23]

[The base, black dress you wear is a sign of a silent and modest person; but if this dress is worn smooth and tight, without a single wrinkle, if you drag it along the ground in order to appear older than you are, if you wear it unstitched or open it to reveal some pleasing part to the eyes of the onlooker, if you wear fitted, shiny, well-polished shoes and your platforms click as if to call attention with every step they take, if your breasts are tightly bound so that they swell and rise upwards to seem rounder and firmer, if you let your hair fall down your back and your locks fall around your temples and breasts, if you ever let your shawl fall from your shoulders to reveal your alabaster neck and back, if suddenly, almost showing that it pains you to have been seen, you hurriedly cover yourself again, if when on the street you cover your face out of shame and then go about all hours revealing and every once in a while showing off what you think will be most pleasing to dishonest eyes, if you do these and other such things pertaining to harlots, do you by chance think you are doing good?]

The structure of this entire passage rests on the conditional "if"; however, the final effect does not suggest a hypothetical portrait. Rather, it offers a detailed description of a widow who resists conforming to the rules of etiquette such as *The Education* defines them. From the clicking of her well-polished platform shoes, or Spanish *chapines*, to her revealing décolleté, this widow epitomizes a fashionable woman in sixteenth-century Spain. The narrator portrays this widow as a fallen woman by calling attention to those things that she literally lets fall such as her dress, her hair and her shawl to reveal those parts of her that are most pleasurable to "dishonest eyes." She falls and quickly covers herself again to produce a dynamic kind of strip tease where her gestures of expert coquetry suggest a high degree of self-awareness. By this account, it is not unfeasible that there existed women in possession of themselves and their own desires during this period. In spite of *The Education*'s condemnation of such a figure—its final question is rhetorical—this passage suggests an enormous power of observation as well as an ability to re-create and lend vitality to what might otherwise represent the most trivial of gestures.

One last question regarding the propriety of remarriage for widows as described in *The Education* bears mention for its relation to the dramatic works where widows play a leading role. *The Education* recognizes that it cannot deny widows the opportunity to contract second nuptials given that such a prohibition represents a heretical stance given marriage's sacramental status. Still, it all but condemns remarriage for widows by considering that those who do so behave like "públicas malas mujeres que venden su cuerpo por acrecentar su hacienda" (evil street women who sell their bodies in order to increase their income).[24] In contrast, widows who forsake a second marriage participate in a kind of "divine knowledge," *divina sabiduría*. The belief that widows should devote themselves to religious works was commonplace during the period, and in this regard, Vives inscribes himself in a line of thinkers who "sought to channel widows' funds to philanthropic ends and to provide the widows themselves with a meaningful lifestyle through church-based activity."[25] It is perhaps not insignificant that such efforts to promote philanthropy were successful; widows often devoted themselves to acts of religious piety such as the founding of religious orders.[26] The seventeenth-century painter Juan Carreño de Miranda (1614–1685), for example, portrays Queen Mariana de Austria wearing the religious habits of her order, thus embodying the religiosity Vives prescribes for widows in *The Education.*

Ideas about remarriage for widows during the early modern period were by no means uniform, and even Vives makes an exception for widows who for reasons of youth, beauty, or poverty find it difficult to abstain from sexual relations.[27] Here, marriage represents the lesser of two evils in a society where sex is considered sinful even *within* the bonds of marriage. This view of sexuality as transgressive, regardless of its presumed sanctification through marriage, raises a number of questions about the role of conjugal relations in early modern Spain. Does the institution of marriage represent a means of social control? Or rather, can it represent an endorsement of sexuality as Vives suggests? At the very least, it is paradoxical that Vives's guide to the *married* life should actually undermine the institution, by disapproving of its sexual dimension, and by extension, discouraging second nuptials for widows.

In contrast to the conduct manuals, the conventions governing the *comedias de enredo* in early modern Spain practically demand a widow's remarriage.[28] In Lope de Vega's *La viuda valenciana* as well as other dramatic works of the period such as Calderón's *La dama duende* and his one-act play or *mojiganga*, *El pésame de la viuda*, widows remarry despite any misgivings they might express at the onset of the dramatic action. They also play an active role in pursuing a new mate suggesting that their initial reservations have more to do with preserving social appearances than any principled opposition to remarriage. For example, when Leonarda, the main protagonist of *La viuda valenciana*, rejects the idea of remarriage after her husband dies, she does so in terms familiar to generations of women who have read *The*

Education published nearly a century earlier. Leonarda's uncle encourages her to contract second nuptials, but she counters:

> ¿A este daño me acomodas
> si todos los que han escrito
> han reprendido infinito
> siempre las segundas bodas?
> La viudez casta y segura
> ¿no es de todos alabada?[29]

> [You encourage me to embrace this danger
> when all who have written
> have always condemned
> second nuptials to an infinite degree?
> Isn't chaste and certain widowhood
> praised by everyone?]

Leonarda rejects her uncle's advice based on the prevailing moral rules that are inscribed in writing and praised by "everyone," and so, the questions she raises here, are simply rhetorical. However, Leonarda's own actions will soon contradict the rules of behavior she espouses in this scene. Soon after she pronounces praise of "chaste and certain widowhood," a gallant, Camilo, catches her eye and leads her to devise an elaborate scheme to consummate her affair without any danger to her sterling reputation as a grieving widow. She maintains this reputation by wearing a mask so that her new lover cannot identify her, even during their most ardent encounters.[30] While such scenes offer the spectator the kind of titillation one might expect from a *comedia de enredo* (and perhaps goes a good deal farther), it also suggests that the social constraints limiting widows' freedom of movement are untenable. Unlike the manuals that presuppose an unambiguous definition of honor, *La viuda* demonstrates that it is difficult, if not impossible, to tell the difference between the appearance of honor and honor itself, for while Leonarda pays lip service to the conventions of widowhood, her actions clearly contradict them.

Lope de Vega dedicates *La viuda valenciana* to Marta de Nevares, addressing her under the pseudonym of Marcia Leonarda. It is not insignificant that the original Marta was herself a recent widow with whom he had maintained adulterous relations.[31] With rare exceptions, critics condemn Lope's dedication with an unusual degree of vitriol.[32] Much of this negative criticism may be attributed to the unapologetic tone Lope's dedication assumes in rejoicing the death of his former rival and Marta's husband, Roque Hernández. Here

Lope's dedication applauds death as a "figura de redentor de la Merced" (figure of Merciful Redemption) with exclamations such as "¡Bien haya la muerte!"(Bravo to death!), and characterizes the recently deceased as ugly, stupid, and jealous.[33] In a surprising reversal of *The Education*'s recommendation that a widow mourn the death of her husband with stoic resignation, Lope's dedication urges her to celebrate the moment.[34] But perhaps what has most vexed critics is what we may refer to as the specific use—or misuse—of literature on Lope's part. In this case, the widow who happens to read or see a performance of *La viuda* discovers how, in fact, she might disregard her husband's death by fully embracing a new lover. In Marta's case, this lover is, of course, Lope.

Regardless of the negative criticism it has received, Lope's dedication and subsequent play represent valuable documents uniting the historical circumstances of his personal life with his dramatic work. Marta de Nevares is acknowledged in *La viuda* because, like her, its main protagonist is recently widowed. As the dedication makes clear, Marta will be able to see her own image "reflected" in the body of the text: "Aquí es donde entra *La viuda valenciana*, espejo en que vuesamerced se tocará mejor que en los cristales de Venecia, y se acordará de mí, que se la dedico" (Here in *The Widow from Valencia* your grace will see herself reflected better than in Venetian crystal, and will remember me as I dedicate it to you).[35] The metaphor of the mirror—an object that will reappear in the play itself—suggests that the artistic material Lope offers Marta de Nevares reflects the real circumstances of their lives rather than an artifact of his own making. He not only elevates *La viuda* to the status of an outstanding work of art by comparing it to a Venetian crystal, but surpasses artifice by endowing his work with the qualities of presumably "real" life.

The dedication invites Marta to identify with the main protagonist of *La viuda* in name, marital status (widow), and behavior, but at the same time it projects an image—or model as Lope would have it—onto its spectator, reader, and in this case, dedicatee. As Frederick A. de Armas suggests, the play provides "answers" to questions Marta might pose, including what actions to take upon her husband's death.[36] Thus, Lope's invitation to Marta to see herself and the circumstances of her life reflected in the fiction of *La viuda* is not necessarily innocent or disinterested. Among other things, it implies that it is possible for her to maintain relations with Lope soon after the death of her husband without serious implications for either of them.[37] Lope suggests that as long as Marta remains "discrete," she can fulfill her desires without suffering any loss to her reputation:

> Discreta fue Leonarda (así los es V. M. y así se llama) en hallar remedio para su soledad, sin empeñar su honor; que como la gala del nadar es saber guardar la ropa, así también lo parece acudir a la voluntad sin faltar a la opinión.[38]

> [Leonarda was discrete (as is your grace and that is what she is called) in discovering a remedy for her solitude, for she did so without pawning her honor; and just as the art of swimming consists of knowing how to keep one's clothes on, so too does fulfilling one's will without loss of reputation.]

Here the abstract notion of honor acquires a material quality; it may be bought and sold, or even temporarily relinquished by "pawning" it. By the same token, this passage warns against the commodification of honor by suggesting that it constitutes a precious good that is cheapened by its very entry into the marketplace of public opinion. These are conventional aspects of honor to which moralists such as Vives would have likely subscribed. What is less conventional is the recognition of a widow's isolation and of her desires, physical or otherwise. By celebrating his protagonist's precautions in fulfilling her desires without losing face, he reveals a loophole to the rules governing widows' behavior. Moreover, this loophole described rather abstractly as the art of swimming without losing one's clothes ("la gala del nadar es saber guarder la ropa"), takes on a literal meaning in the play when Leonarda consummates her desire without removing her mask. She does not lose face as long as her identity remains hidden from those who have the most to gain from exposing her, in this case, Camilo. Thus, much of the suspense in *La viuda valenciana* centers on how long Leonarda can maintain the charade before she is discovered.

Lope's dedication to Marta de Nevares not only acknowledges widows' isolation but defines it as problematic. Rather than condemn widows to perpetual isolation, Lope offers his public—including the widows among them—a new moral code.[39] By this code, honor possesses a relative value that is not only subject to public opinion, but also to personal prerogatives. According to the conduct manuals, a husband's death virtually ends wife's participation in society, for what had defined her place in it—that is her husband—ceases to exist. *La viuda valenciana* offers an alternative view to that of the marriage manuals by suggesting that a husband's death may, in fact, release her from the obligations she incurs at the moment of her betrothal in order to pursue her freedom outside the domestic sphere. And while this freedom is brief, it is not negligible given that it permits Leonarda to break her solitary confinement in order to maintain a liaison with Camilo.

Early in the play, Leonarda reveals her desire to escape the dark and isolation to which she is subject as a widow in a simple, short utterance:

"Ya quiero sol" (Now I want the sun).[40] Light and life stand in opposition of darkness and death, although for a brief moment she claims to follow the more difficult path of mourning and self-sacrifice: "en la dificultad / escriben que está la gloria" (it is written that there is greater glory in overcoming hardship).[41] As a devoted widow, literature is the only pleasure in which she indulges, a pastime she characterizes as safe since it does not put her reputation at risk. Moreover, her devotion to reading is directly related to her refusal to remarry:

> como he dado en no casarme,
> leo por entretenerme,
> no por bachillera hacerme,
> y de aguda graduarme;
> que a quien su buena opinión
> encierra en silencio tal,
> no halla en los libros mal.
> Gustosa conversación
> es cualquier libro discreto,
> que si cansa, de hablar deja,
> es amigo que aconseja
> y reprehende en secreto.
> Al fin, después que los leo
> y trato de devoción,
> de alguna imaginación
> voy castigando el deseo.[42]

> [Since I've decided not to marry,
> I read for fun,
> rather than to become a bachelor
> or to receive a degree in cleverness.
> Anyone who seeks a good reputation
> in this cloistered silence
> will not find harm in books.
> Any discrete book
> provides delicious conversation;
> if it's tiresome, it stops talking,
> like a friend who gives advice
> and scolds you in secret.
> In short, ever since I started
> reading and treating pious subjects
> I keep my desires at bay
> by means of the imagination.]

In Leonarda's eloquent praise of reading, it is clear that literature stands as a substitute for other pleasures. Although she confines her readings to religious works—in the first scene she asks her servant to bring her a book by "Fray Luis"—the above passage makes plain that she does not seek moral or intellectual edification through her readings.[43] She consciously distances herself from the *culta latiniparlas*—the female characters whose linguistic excesses Lope parodies in *La dama boba*—although she shares their distaste for marriage. However, while the *culta latiniparla* rejects marriage out of devotion to intellectual pursuits, Leonarda does not provide another, presumably higher cause. By her own admission, she does not seek to emulate the exemplary widows of the past such as Artemisa who went to such extremes as to drink the ashes of her dead husband.[44] Much less does she forsake a second marriage in order to perform the kind of religious works advocated by Vives. When Leonarda states in perfunctory terms that she will not remarry ("he dado en no casarme"), the spectator is not given to understand that anything but an attachment to her status as a single woman motivates her: "Quiero ser una mujer, / que, como es razón, acuda / al título de vïuda, / pues a nadie he menester" (I want to be a woman / who, since it is true, can claim / a widow's title / as I need nothing from no one).[45] It is arguably this lack of a moral or religious motivation paired with a sense of self-reliance that marks Leonarda as decidedly modern in her sensibilities.

Regardless of Leonarda's reasons for reading, she soon abandons her books in order to pursue other, more carnal pleasures. She asks her maid to bring her a painting; instead, the maid brings her a mirror so that her mistress might contemplate her own beauty in order to reflect on what she is missing by leading a life of strict seclusion. It is a brief but striking scene given the broader context of Lope's dedication to Marta de Nevares where he invites her to see herself in the "mirror" of the text. In the play's action the order is reversed,—the maid offers Leonarda an actual mirror instead of a work of art—but at stake in both the dedication and in this scene are the ephemeral qualities of youth and beauty. Just as Lope encourages Marta to celebrate the moment of her husband's death, so too the maid encourages Leonarda to recognize and act on her considerable physical charms. The play itself will demonstrate what can happen if Leonarda does not act on her desires while she is still in possession of her youth.

Toward the conclusion, Camilo mistakes an old woman for Leonarda. Thinking that she is, in fact, the person with whom he has maintained a number of secret trysts, Camilo reacts with revulsion by penning a sonnet to this "vieja de Satanás" (Satanic old woman) in which he refuses to continue seeing her.[46] Mistaken identities are, of course, part and parcel of the comedy of errors, but this particular case also serves as a warning to those overzealous guardians of young women, including the women themselves. The attention Leonarda craves from Camilo is lost at the moment he believes that he has been duped by an old woman whom he caricatures in his sonnet: "antigua cara con dobleces / tiznadas cejas y canudos rizos, / con la tuerta nariz, dientes postizos" (an ancient wrinkled face, / blackened brows and grey curls / a crooked nose and false teeth).[47] In this sonnet, Camilo rejects what he has previously—and passionately—embraced, or at least groped in the dark. The underlying message of this scene suggests that Leonarda cannot expect for her overtures to be reciprocated by the likes of Camilo once she has reached senectitude.

This message exhorting Leonarda to reap the fruits of her youth and beauty constitutes a commonplace of Spanish letters most famously rendered in Garcilaso de la Vega's sonnet "En tanto que de rosa y azucena." It also stands in direct contradiction to the chaste behavior women are presumed to observe during the period as the didactic literature on marriage makes plain. In this regard, Leonarda represents one of the staunchest defenders of this contradiction, that is, she simultaneously protects her reputation while following the dictates of *carpe diem*. In order to pursue an affair with him, she stipulates that he cannot, under any circumstances, discover her true identity as it would put her reputation at risk. Thus, she is able to achieve a temporary reconciliation of the contrary forces that demand she preserve her reputation and, at the same time, take pleasure in the joys of youth.

While this reconciliation may be read as Leonarda's submission to the contradictions that reduce women to either chaste or unchaste subjects, another, perhaps more persuasive interpretation, is that she refuses to be held to a single standard of morality, particularly one in which prudery plays a dominant role. For if Leonarda derives pleasure from her secret encounters with Camilo, the spectator is not led to believe that she does so out of fear of getting old and thus losing the attention of her paramour, even though such a possibility is realized the moment Camilo mistakes an old woman for Leonarda. Rather, throughout the play there is the sense that the young widow revels in satisfying her desires outside the confines of marriage. While such a marriage would—and at the conclusion of the play does, in fact, legitimate her affair—it nonetheless revokes her cherished status as a widow. However, the patently absurd premise of the conditions Leonarda imposes on Camilo render it difficult for her to sustain the charade by which he must literally be kept in the dark each and every time he is in her company.

Leonarda's uncle, Lucencio plays a primarily paternal role in the play, and while he might be expected to advocate his niece's cloistered life, he in fact chastises her when he discovers that she refuses to look in a mirror, because she considers it frivolous behavior. He attributes her excesses to her capricious nature: "A enojo siempre me incito / con tu melindre estremado" (My anger is always provoked / by your excessive whims).[48] In a curious anecdote, he contrasts her refusal to look in any mirror with the excessive vanity of women who dwell on their reflection even as they are being courted. Rather than gaze at their Romeos from their windows, these women admire themselves in small mirrors that pass undetected:

> junto a las celosías
> hacen colgar muchos días
> su espejo, o en medio dellas;
> y así como están hablando
> por defuera a su galán,
> el habla y meneos van
> en el espejo mirando;
> y el necio a quien satisface,
> por sí lo entiende y se admira;
> y es el espejo a quien mira,
> a quien la fiesta se hace.[49]

> [they hang a mirror for several days
> next to or in the middle of the shutters,
> and while speaking
> to their suitor outside, they
> gaze at their own words and gestures
> in the mirror.
> The fool who they satisfy
> believes he is the one
> to whom they listen and admire,
> when it's the mirror she
> sees and celebrates.]

In the broader context of the play whereby the work of art represents a kind of metaphorical mirror, Lucencio's story presents itself as a warning. It suggests that by identifying too closely with a work of art, the spectator may forget that any characters appearing in *La viuda* are fictitious and that any resemblance to real persons, living or dead is purely coincidental. One may ask if Lucencio's words also serve as a warning to the critic who takes offense at Lope's dedication to Marta. At the very least, it suggests that the spectator not take this comedy too seriously for otherwise he risks being taken for a fool, just like the suitor who is unaware that the true object of his lover's devotion is her own image.[50]

It is significant that the paternal figure in *La viuda valenciana* urges Leonarda to remarry given that the treatises advise against second nuptials. His recommendations represent a surprising reversal from the morality espoused by moralists such as Vives and Fray Luis de León. Nonetheless, the terms of the debate between Leonarda and her uncle are not unfamiliar since they place her reputation squarely in the center of the discussion. On the one hand, she argues against contracting a second marriage in order to protect her reputation as a widow. She adds a colorful list of reasons against marriage, including a detailed and imaginative description of a *"lindo,"* or dandy whose excessive attention to his appearance leads him to squander her dowry.[51] On the other hand, Lucencio argues that it is precisely her refusal to contract second nuptials that puts her reputation at risk. He argues that no amount of seclusion can protect her from "la invidia y vulgo vil," that is, from envy and a "vile" public. Like Leonarda, his imagination leads him to create the precise image of her downfall; according to Lucencio, the public will assume that she is maintaining illicit relations with a slave.[52]

By conspiring to destroy Leonarda's reputation, the trio of suitors that court her over the course of the play's action confirms Lucencio's worse fears.[53] Otón, Valerio, and Lisandro appear throughout the course of the action, and together they suggest a parody of their serious classical counterparts, the Greek chorus. Their utter failure to seduce Leonarda, their accusation of Urban, whom they suspect of maintaining relations with his mistress, and finally, their botched attempt to kill him, results in their farcical presence in *La viuda valenciana*. Above all, they bring disrepute to themselves through their unsuccessful attempts to slander the young widow, an activity in which they take genuine, if perverse, pleasure, confirmed by the exclamation, "¡Qué dulce es el murmurar!" (How sweet it is to gossip!).[54] The precise nature of this slander centers on her status as a widow. According to all three of them, it is inconceivable that Leonarda leads an existence independent of a man:

> Viuda, ya no hay quien crea
> que estáis sin dueño secreto
> del alma, porque en efeto

andáis triste y no sois fea.
Mujer bella, rica y moza
—que basta libre y mujer—,
yo no tengo de creer
que no se regala y goza.[55]

[Widow, no one believes
you do not have a secret soul mate
because you, in fact,
appear sad, and yet you are not ugly.
I cannot believe a beautiful, rich, and young woman
—suffice to say a free woman—
does not indulge and take her pleasure.]

The fact that Leonarda does, in fact, possess a "dueño secreto" or secret lover is, in many ways, irrelevant, for Otón, Valerio, and Lisandro appear far more ridiculous for their suspicions than she does for confirming them. She successfully orchestrates her affairs without their knowledge, and it is arguably her ability to outwit them at every turn that represents one of the main sources of delight in the play.

Camilo, who is understandably desperate to discover his lover's identity, brings out a light and succeeds in discovering that it is, in fact, Leonarda with whom he has maintained a secret affair. It is only at this moment that her charade comes to an abrupt end, and just as abruptly, she proposes that they marry: "Si fuere voluntad suya / yo quiero ser su mujer" (If it is his will / I want to be his wife).[56] Leonarda claims that mutual attraction as opposed to any adherence to social decorum have drawn them together: "quiéreme bien, y también / yo a él por el mismo estilo" (he loves me and I also / love him in the same way).[57] This statement is a bold one if we consider that Camilo has, only seconds before, learned who Leonarda actually is; until now, he has known her in an exclusively carnal sense. Theirs is a one-sided affair, in that he does not possess even basic knowledge about her, including her name or age. If they love each other as she claims, then this love is based on the physical nature of their encounters that she suggests constitute a valuable preamble to marriage. This is an astonishing suggestion for the period given the moralists' admonitions against premarital relations between the sexes.

Apart from Leonarda's declarations of mutual attraction, the only note of irony in this scene occurs at the moment her servant lets her previous three suitors into her home to witness her engagement to Camilo. At the moment they enter, she asks this servant, "¿Por qué un pueblo no llamabas, / o media ciudad traías?" (Why didn't you bring the whole town / or half the city?).[58] Despite her uncle's claim that the comic trio of suitors deserve to stand as witnesses given their status as "honorable gentlemen," the legitimacy of her complaint clearly outweighs any reason for their presence. In the end, however, Leonarda is defeated only insofar as the shroud of privacy surrounding her affair with Camilo has been torn asunder. There is little else to suggest that Leonarda has been prevented from fulfilling her desires, even though she must do so surreptiously. She actively pursues Camilo on her own terms over the course of the action and contracts marriage of her own free will. Just as importantly, she is unapologetic at the moment she confesses her "love" for him, carnal or otherwise. There is therefore much to suggest that Leonarda ends *La viuda valenciana* on a triumphant note.

The distance separating *La viuda valenciana* from the precepts governing widows' behavior could hardly be greater. If Leonarda attends to these precepts, she does so in name only given that she exercises extraordinary agency throughout the play. In sharp contrast to Vives's rules governing widows' behavior, she refuses to live a life of strict seclusion and participates in all manner of activities considered off-limits to widows by embracing a lover, even if only in the dark. *La viuda valenciana* therefore does little to alleviate the anxiety that the "potentially unfettered sexual longing" of the widow might produce in Spanish society.[59] On the contrary, this potential is unleashed and given unusually free rein on the stage for the delight of those members of the public that do not share Vives's strict sense of morality.

Notes

1. Covarrubias, *Tesoro de la lengua castellana o española*, 217. Marjo Buitelaar notes that "In Latin and Greek there is no masculine form to match the term 'widow,' while in the Anglo-Saxon language a masculine form only appeared in the late fourteenth century." Buitelaar, "Widow's Worlds," 4.

2. Hufton, 42.

3. Brundage, *Law, Sex, and Christian Society in Medieval Europe*, 563–65, 574–75.

4. In Erika Rummel's edition of Erasmus's writings on women, she warns against the potential pitfalls of works such as *In Praise of Marriage*: "Clearly such pieces were meant to provide a collection of commonplaces rather than an expression of the author's views. Erasmus himself points out the rhetorical nature of such works. For example in his *In Praise of Marriage* he notes that it belongs to the genre of declamations, which 'deal with imaginary subjects for the purpose of exercising one's ingenuity . . . ; the nature of these exercises is to treat the argument from both sides."

Erasmus, *Erasmus on Women*, 4. Still, Rummel considers that such works "do not invalidate their use as sources of social history; they merely prevent us from ascribing the views expressed specifically to Erasmus." Erasmus, Erasmus on Women. More importantly, Erasmus's other works on the subject of marriage confirm the views expressed in this "example of a letter of persuasion." Ibid., 129.

5. Studies of particular relevance include Maxime Chevalier's chapter on the literary figure of the widow in *Tipos cómicos y folkore (siglos XVI–XVII)*, Louise O. Vasvari's "Why Is Doña Endrina a Widow? Traditional Culture and Textuality in the *LBA*," and Juan Carlos Ramírez Pimienta's "La aventura de doña Endrina y don Melón de la Uerta: El matrimonio de la viuda como control social." Philip O. Gericke examines a very different but no less valuable representation of the widow in "The Widow in Hispanic Balladry: *Fonte Frida*." In this ballad, the widow's suffering leads her to reject, rather than accommodate a new mate.

6. Chevalier, *Tipos cómicos y folklore (siglos XVI–XVII)*, 86, and Vasvari, "Why Is Doña Endrina a Widow? Traditional Culture and Textuality in the *Libro de buen amor*," 262–63.

7. Brundage, "Widows as Disadvantaged Persons in Medieval Canon Law," 194.

8. Ratcliffe, "Así que donde no hay varón, todo bien fallece," 311.

9. In reference to the social history of women during the Enlightenment, Olwen Hufton suggests that "an abundance of evidence indicates that wealthy widows thrived when their husbands died." Hufton, 42. Most of the examples Hufton offers are drawn from eighteenth-century British and French sources; however, in "Widows in the Chronicles of Late Medieval Castile," Clara Estow refers to royal Spanish widows who were "able to assume a persona independent from her spouse, and . . . to command, at least for a time, the attention of the realm." Estow, "Widows in the Chronicles of Late Medieval Castile," 164. Manuel Fernández Álvarez observes that in Spain widows could occupy positions of special privilege: "A las viudas se les podía confiar puestos que en ningún modo hubieran podido obtener las solteras ni las casadas. Carlos V piensa en su hermana María y la nombra Gobernadora de los Países Bajos porque tiene esa autoridad social que comportaba su viudez. Y algo similar ocurriría años después con Margarita de Parma. Juana de Austria sería Gobernadora de Castilla en 1554 porque ya era viuda del príncipe Juan Manuel de Portugal" (Widows could be entrusted with positions that could in no way would have been obtained by single or married women. Charles V thinks in his sister María and names her Governor of the Low Countries because she possesses the social authority conferred by her widowhood. And something similar occurs years later with Margarita de Parma. Juana de Austria would be Governor of Castille in 1554 because she was the widow of the prince Juan Manuel de Portugal). Fernández Álvarez, *Casadas, monjas, rameras y brujas*, 126.

10. Ruiz, *Libro de buen amor*, lines 581–82.

11. Ruiz, *The Book of Good Love*, line 581–82.

12. Buitelaar, "Widow's Worlds," 7.

13. Vives, *Instrucción de la mujer cristiana*, 441.

14. Vives, *The Education of a Christian Woman*, 8.

15. Vives, *Instrucción de la mujer cristiana*, 351.

16. Ibid., 379.

17. Ibid.

18. For example, Jodi Bilinkoff states that "research on early modern Italy, Spain, and Spanish America reveals that female founders and patrons of religious institutions were virtually always widows. This strong correlation suggests that religious patronage represented a socially and culturally acceptable way for widows to invest their resources, as well as one that proved meaningful to them as individuals." Bilinkoff, "Elite Widows and Religious Expression in Early Modern Spain: The View from Avila," 183.

19. Vives, *Instrucción de la mujer cristiana*, 373. Vives, *The Education of a Christian Woman*, 315.

20. Vives, *Instrucción de la mujer cristiana*, 376. Vives, *The Education of a Christian Woman*, 317.

21. Ruiz, *The Book of Good Love*, line 582.

22. Vives holds in contempt a woman who does not love her husband: "Harto largamente declaramos en el libro pasado que la mujer que no ama a su marido como a sí misma no es merecedora de ser llamada mujer." Vives, *Instrucción de la mujer cristiana*, 354.

23. Ibid., 380.

24. Ibid., 388.

25. Hufton, 43.

26. Ibid. See also Buitelaar, "Widow's Worlds," 2, and Bilinkoff, "Elite Widows and Religious Expression in Early Modern Spain: The View from Avila," 181–92.

27. Vives invokes a commonplace of the period whereby it is better for widows to marry than to "burn" with desire: "Pero si por ser moza, o hermosa o pobre, por cualquier otro respeto, teme de no poderse contener, ni guarder su castidad, oiga lo que dice el apóstol a los de Corinto: 'Digo a las casadas y viudas que harán bien permanecer en el estamento de vida que Nuestro Señor las ha puesto, como yo hago en el mío, o si no, ayúntense por vía de matrimonio, porque mejor es casarse que arder'" (But if she is young, beautiful or poor, or for any other reason, is afraid she cannot restrain herself or guard her chastity, listen to what the apostole says in the Corinthians: 'I say to the wives and widows that they will do well to remain in the station of life that our Lord has placed them, as I stay in mine, and if not, join in marriage, because it is better to marry than to burn'). Vives, *Instrucción de la mujer cristiana*, 389.

28. For a definition of the *comedia de capa y espada*, see Bruce Wardropper's "La comedia española en el Siglo de Oro," as well as Ignacio Arrellano's "Convenciones y rasgos genéricos en la comedia de capa y espada."

29. Vega, *La viuda valenciana*, line 54.

30. The production of *La viuda valenciana* by the Teatres de la Generalitat Valenciana directed by Vicente Genovés in 2008 emphasizes the mask's centrality on its poster by placing a richly ornamented purple and gold Venetian mask in its center.

31. Ferrer Valls, "La viuda valenciana de Lope de Vega o el arte de nadar y guardar la ropa," 2.

32. José Luis Aguirre characterizes the dedication as "exultante de salvaje alegría, vitalidad y mal gusto" (overjoyed by savage happiness, vitality, and bad taste). Quoted in de Armas, "Mujer y mito en el teatro clásico español," 62. Jaime Fernández refers to its "immorality" and adds that "Lope gives examples, of rudeness, savageness, and vileness and a lack of compassion and pity." Fernández, "Honor y moralidad en La viuda valenciana de Lope de Vega," 821. Frederick de Armas's study of *La viuda valenciana* offers an alternative interpretation of the play's presumed "immorality": "Although Lope's joy at the death of Marta's husband is shocking, I do not believe that Lope demonstrates a 'provocation of the public's judgment' as Castro and Rennert believe. . . . Rather, the poet wants to offer his public a new type of morality based on an Neo-Platonic ideal of love that transcends the laws of the period." de Armas, "Mujer y mito en el teatro clásico español," 62–63.

33. Vega, *La viuda valenciana*, 39.

34. As Teresa Ferrer Valls asserts, "Lope compares Marta de Nevares' marriage with an imprisonment and her widowhood with liberation." Ferrer Valls, "La viuda valenciana de Lope de Vega o el arte de nadar y guardar la ropa," 20.

35. Vega, La viuda valenciana, 38–39.

36. de Armas, "Mujer y mito en el teatro clásico español," 61–62.

37. Frederick A. de Armas observes: "When Marta de Nevares asks if she should marry after the death of her husband, Lope shows her how to 'remedy her solitude without pawning her honor' . . . that is, how to continue loving Lope without marrying him." Ibid., 62.

38. Vega, *La viuda valenciana*, 91.

39. de Armas, "Mujer y mito en el teatro clásico español," 63.

40. Vega, *La viuda valenciana*, line 653.

41. Ibid., lines 109–10.

42. Ibid., lines 29–45.

43. According to Teresa Ferrer Valls, this reference is likely to Fray Luis de Granada's *Libro de la oración y meditación*. Ferrer Valls, "La viuda valenciana de Lope de Vega o el arte de nadar y guardar la ropa," 29.

44. Vega, *La viuda valenciana*, lines 69–72.

45. Ibid., lines 81–84.

46. Ibid., line 2697.

47. Ibid., 2701–4.

48. Ibid., lines 143–44.

49. Ibid., lines 153–64.

50. For some of the problems involved in analyzing comic works of the period, see Arellano, *Historia del teatro español del siglo XVII*, 131–39.

51. Vega, *La viuda valenciana*, lines 253–96.

52. Ibid., lines 225–28.

53. In the introduction to her edition of *La viuda Valencia*, Teresa Ferrer Valls remarks on the role of these three characters: "Leonarda's trio of suitors protagonizes, for its part, a good number of comic situations and represents the social judgment that Lucencio had feared so much." Ibid., 51.

54. Ibid., line 1744.

55. Ibid., lines 1601–8.

56. Vega, *Peribáñez and the Comendador*, lines 2927–28.

57. Vega, *La viuda valenciana*, lines 2925–26.

58. Ibid., lines 2941–42.

59. Buitelaar, "Widow's Worlds," 7.

Conclusion

Pensarán que está acabada
la comedia con casarse
los galanes y las damas
que otro pedacito falta.

—Pedro Calderón de la Barca, Los empeños de un acaso

The formulaic endings of the *comedia* might lead us to believe that conjugal relations in early modern Spain conform to the morality spelled out decades earlier in the treatises devoted to marriage. If there are discernable patterns whereby tragedy ends in the violent dissolution of marriage and comedy concludes in the felicitous union of the couple, upon closer examination, the path leading to and from the altar is far more circuitous and less predictable than might first appear.[1] It is a route befitting the Baroque aesthetic of unexpected and often violent twists and turns, where Renaissance ideals of balance and reciprocity give way to imbalance and discord. In the *comedia*'s embrace of the Baroque aesthetic, a space for conflict emerges, particularly conjugal conflicts in which both men and women play active, and often antagonistic, roles. Whereas the didactic literature on marriage exhorts women to be silent and subservient to whomever happens to act as the patriarchal figure in their lives, the dramatic literature paints a very different picture. Women are neither static nor voiceless characters, but rather eloquent advocates for the exercise of free will. They may or may not be successful in this exercise, but their voices stand as a testament of their vibrant presence on the early modern Spanish stage.

This stage therefore represents one of the most conspicuous spaces in which ideas of self-determination are allowed to unfold, challenging the moralists' strict definitions of marriage. Few topics relating to conjugal matters, including many considered taboo by the standards of the period, are left untouched by the likes of Lope, Cervantes, and Calderón, as they transform the ordinary experience of married life into the extraordinary stuff of drama. In these dramatists' works, the institution of marriage and its attendant rituals of courtship, betrothal, and consummation, receive as much attention as those experiences that act to sever the conjugal bond, including adultery, divorce, and widowhood. Above all, the public in seventeenth-century Spain possesses an acute hunger for "los casos de la honra" (cases involving honor), as Lope was well aware.[2] In this regard, one of the greatest ironies of the dramatization of conjugal relations during this period is that the theater, the space that epitomizes public space, should represent some of the most intensely private moments of human relations. It may, in fact, be the public dimension of the stage that invites the artist to expose the private sources of shame in early modern Spain, including "impure" blood, *converso* origins, and infidelity.

Unlike the prescriptive literature devoted to marriage, the *comedia* does not necessarily enforce the moral codes governing honor. Instead of exhorting the spectator to uphold the values associated with conjugal honor at any price, the *comedia* often represents these values as constantly shifting, unstable, and potentially destructive forces. While the formulaic nature of the *comedia* demands that tragedy fulfill honor's destructive potential and comedy avoid it, many of the most exceptional dramatic works of this period offer the spectator hybrid resolutions to conflict that do not conform to the demands of genre, much less to the demands of conventional morality. The constant censure of the theater by the moralists stands as persuasive evidence of the *comedias'* powers of provocation. If the *comedia* presupposes a number of formulaic conventions, it contradicts them just as often in order to create dynamic works that are far less predictable and more modern in their sensibility than the prescriptive literature devoted to regulating conjugal behavior.

Further research into other works by these writers included in this study, as well as the works of other dramatists of the period, is likely to confirm Lope's disregard of moral and artistic conventions in favor of the public's demands for compelling drama. In *El arte nuevo de hacer comedias en este tiempo* (*The New Art of Writing Plays in This Time*) of 1609, Lope exhorts his fellow dramatists to choose their subject without excessive concern for the rules governing the drama up until that moment: "Elíjase el sujeto y no se mire, / (perdonen los preceptos) si es de reyes" (Choose the subject and do not consider, / [pardon the precepts] if it is of kings).[3] Lope's dramas, as well as those of his contemporaries, do just that when it comes to the subject of marriage, that is, they forgo the precepts that might have prevented them from including cuckolds, libertines, and adulterers on the stage. But these dramatists do more than include a colorful cast of characters in their dramas; by breaking with the aesthetic conventions that had governed the drama until that moment, they present a compelling case for the exercise of free will in both personal and artistic matters.

In the epigram at the beginning of this discussion, the "gracioso" or fool warns the spectator the action is not quite over, even though "los galanes y las damas" (the gallants and the ladies) in the play have already contracted marriage. This small but significant gesture calls attention to the mechanisms governing the *comedia*, whereby nuptials typically mark the "happy end" of the dramatic action. By casting an ironic gaze on the formulas governing the *comedia* this character points to the artifice underlying the staging of marriage in early modern Spain, and by extension, exposes the fiction whereby marriage *necessarily* plays a predetermined role in people's lives. The invitation to wait just a bit longer for the play to conclude not only represents a case of delayed gratification, but also an opportunity to reflect on the role of human agency in marriage. Despite political, economic, and religious constraints, the desire to determine one's own fate in personal matters, particularly conjugal matters, begins to play a greater role than had been allowed for until this moment in Spain's history.

Notes

1. "Based on the . . . notion of marriage as closure, early modern Spanish comic theater reveals its other dimensions, not merely its propagandistic complicity in promoting marriage as a social structure of the patriarchal orders. Social hegemony functions as a process of struggle between and among forces, not merely as a confirmation of the dominant orders. Hence, the rites of passage found in the concluding marriage scene are social as well as artistic forms that both confirm social orders and allow for their problematization on stage or off." Connor, "Marriage and Subversion in Comedia Endings," 31. Connor's analysis may be extended to include tragic works insofar that they also represent an unequivocal "struggle between and among forces."

2. Vega, *Arte nuevo de hacer comedias*, line 327.

3. Ibid., lines 157–58.

Works Cited

Alcalá, Angel. "Pecularidad de las acusaciones a fray Luis en el marco del proceso a sus colegas salmantinos." Pp. 65–80 in *Fray Luis de León: Historia, humanismo y letras*, edited by Víctor García de la Concha and Javier San José Lera. Salamanca: Ediciones Universidad de Salamanca, 1996.

———. *Proceso inquisitorial de Fray Luis de León: Edición paleográfica, anotada y crítica.* Junta de Castilla y León: Consejería de Cultura y Turismo, 1991.

Arellano, Ignacio. *Historia del teatro español del siglo XVII.* Madrid: Cátedra, 1995.

de Armas, Frederick A. "Mujer y mito en el teatro clásico español: *La viuda valenciana* y *La dama duende.*" *Lenguaje y Textos* 3 (1993): 57–72.

Austin, J. L. *How to Do Things with Words: Second Edition.* Cambridge, MA: Harvard University Press, 1975.

Bataillon, Marcel. *Erasmo y España: Estudios sobre la historia espiritual del siglo XVI.* México: Fondo de Cultura Económica, 1966.

———. *Varia lección de clásicos españoles.* Madrid: Gredos, 1964.

Benabu, Isaac. "'Who Is the Protagonist?': Gutierre on the Stand." *Indiana Journal of Hispanic Literatures* 2, no. 2 (1994): 13–25.

Benjamin, Walter. *The Origin of German Tragic Drama.* London and New York: Verso, 1998.

Bennassar, Bartolomé. *L'Inquisition espagnole, XVe–XIXe Siècle,* 1979.

———. *Los españoles: actitudes y mentalidad desde el s. XVI al s. XIX,* translated by Araceli de la Encina Pascua. San Lorenzo de El Escorial (Madrid): Swan, 1985.

Bilinkoff, Jodi. "Elite Widows and Religious Expression in Early Modern Spain: The View from Avila." In *Widowhood in Medieval and Early Modern Europe,* edited by Sandra Cavallo and Lyndan Warner. New York: Longman, 1999.

Boorman, John T. "Divina Ley and Derecho Humano in *Peribáñez*." *Bulletin of the Comediantes* 12, no. 2 (1960): 12–14.

Bravo Arriaga, María Dolores. "Los entremeses cervantinos, valores sociales y risa crítica: El retablo de las maravillas." Pp. 141–48 in *Dramaturgia española y novo-hispana (siglos XVI–XVII)*, edited by Lillian von der Walde Moheno and Serafín González García. Iztapalapa, México, D.F.: Universidad Autónoma Metropolitana, Unidad Iztapalapa, 1993.

Brundage, James A. *Law, Sex, and Christian Society in Medieval Europe*. Chicago: University of Chicago Press, 1987.

———. "Widows as Disadvantaged Persons in Medieval Canon Law." Pp. 193–206 in *Upon My Husband's Death: Widows in the Literature and Histories of Medieval Europe*, edited by Louise Mirrer. Ann Arbor: University of Michigan Press, 1992.

Buitelaar, Marjo. "Widow's Worlds." In *Between Poverty and the Pyre: Moments in the History of Widowhood*, edited by Jan N. Bremmer and Laurens van den Bosch. London and New York: Routledge, 1995.

Calderón de la Barca, Pedro. *El médico de su honra*, edited by Don Cruickshank. Madrid: Castalia, 1989.

———. *La vida es sueño*, edited by Ciriaco Morón Arroyo. Madrid: Catédra, 2001.

———. *Life Is a Dream*. London: N. Hern Books, 1998.

———. *The Surgeon of His Honour*, translated by Roy Campbell. Westport, CT: Greenwood Press, 1978.

Castilla, Alberto. "El arte teatral de Calderón en *El médico de su honra*." Pp. 403–12 in *Calderón: Actas del congreso internacional sobre Calderón y el teatro español del siglo de oro: Madrid, 8–13 de junio de 1981*, edited by Luciano García Lorenzo. Madrid: Consejo Superior de Investigaciones Científicas, 1983.

Cavell, Stanley. *Pursuits of Happiness the Hollywood Comedy of Remarriage*. Cambridge, MA: Harvard University Press, 1981.

Cervantes Saavedra, Miguel de. *Don Quixote*, translated by Walter Starkie. New York: Signet Classic, 2001.

———. *El ingenioso hidalgo don Quijote de la Mancha*. Madrid: Castalia, 1991.

———. *Entremeses*, edited by Nicholas Spadaccini. Madrid: Cátedra, 1982.

———. *The Interludes of Cervantes*, translated by Griswold S. Morley. Princeton, NJ: Princeton University Press, 1948.

Chevalier, Maxime. *Tipos cómicos y folklore (siglos XVI–XVII)*. Madrid: EDI-6, 1982.

Connor, Catherine. "Marriage and Subversion in Comedia Endings: Problems in Art and Society." Pp. 23–46 in *Gender, Identity, and Representation in Spain's Golden Age*, edited by Dawn L. Smith and Anita K. Stoll. Lewisburg, PA: Bucknell University Press, 2000.

Coontz, Stephanie. *Marriage, a History: How Love Conquered Marriage*. New York: Penguin Books, 2006.

Correa, Gustavo. "El doble aspecto de la honra en *Peribáñez y el comendador de Ocaña*." *Hispanic Review* 26, no. 3 (July 1958): 188–99.

Cotarelo y Mori, Emilio. *Bibliografía de las controversias sobre la licitud del teatro en España*, edited by José Luis Suárez García. Granada: Universidad de Granada, 1997.

Covarrubias, Sebastián de. *Tesoro de la lengua castellana o española*, edited by Martín de Riquer. Barcelona: Alta Fulla, 1998.

Cruickshank, Don William. *Calderón de la Barca, El médico de su honra*. London: Grant & Cutler, 2003.

Cruz, Anne J. "Deceit, Desire, and the Limits of Subversion in Cervantes's Interludes." *Cervantes: Bulletin of the Cervantes Society of America* 14, no. 2 (1994): 119–36.

Culler, Jonathan D. *The Pursuit of Signs: Semiotics, Literature, Deconstruction*. Ithaca, NY: Cornell University Press, 2002.

Davis, Natalie Zemon. *The Return of Martin Guerre*. Cambridge, MA: Harvard University Press, 1983.

Defourneaux, Marcelin. *La vida cotidiana en la España del siglo de oro*. Barcelona: Argos Vergara, 1983.

Delgado-Morales, Manuel. "Palabra y ornato en la puesta en escena de *Peribáñez y Fuenteovejuna*." *Hispanic Review* 61, no. 3 (1993): 345–61.

Duby, Georges. *Love and Marriage in the Middle Ages*. Chicago: University of Chicago Press, 1994.

Dunn, P. N. "Honour and the Christian Background in Calderón." *Bulletin of Hispanic Studies* 37 (1960): 75–105.

Durán, Manuel. *Luis de Léon*. New York: Twayne Publishers, 1971.

Eco, Umberto. "Semiotics of Theatrical Performance." *Tulane Drama Review* 21, no. 1 (1977): 107–17.

Egido, Aurora. "La vida es sueño y los idiomas del silencio." Pp. 229–44 in *Homenaje al Profesor Antonio Vilanova*, edited by Adolfo Sotelo Vázquez. Barcelona: Departamento de Filología Española, Facultad de Filología, División de Ciencias Humanas y Sociales, Universidad de Barcelona, 1989.

Elliott, John Huxtable. *Imperial Spain 1469–1716*. London: Penguin, 2002.

Erasmus, Desiderius. *Collected Works of Erasmus*. Toronto: University of Toronto Press, 1974.

———. *Erasmus on Women*. Toronto: University of Toronto Press, 1996.

———. *The Colloquies of Erasmus*, translated by Craig S. Thompson. Chicago: University of Chicago Press, 1965.

Esteban Mateo, León. *Hombre-Mujer en Vives: Itinerario para la reflexión*. Valencia: Ajuntament de València, 1994.

Estow, Clara. "Widows in the Chronicles of Late Medieval Castile." Pp. 153–65 in *Upon My Husband's Death: Widows in the Literature and Histories of Medieval Europe*, edited by Louise Mirrer. Ann Arbor: University of Michigan Press, 1992.

Evans, Peter. "*Peribáñez* and Ways of Looking at Golden Age Dramatic Characters." *Romanic Review* 74, no. 2 (March 1983): 136–51.

Fernández Álvarez, Manuel. *Casadas, monjas, rameras y brujas: La olvidada historia de la mujer española en el renacimiento*. Madrid: Espasa, 2002.

Fernández, Jaime. "Honor y moralidad en *La viuda valenciana* de Lope de Vega: 'Un tan indigno ejemplo.'" *Hispania: A Journal Devoted to the Teaching of Spanish and Portuguese* 69, no. 4 (December 1986): 821–29.

Ferrer Valls, Teresa. "*La viuda valenciana* de Lope de Vega o el arte de nadar y guardar la ropa." Pp. 15 in *Cuadernos de teatro clásico*, edited by V. E. Kohler and L. et Bandello. Madrid: Compañia Nacional de Teatro Clásico, 1999.

Fischer, Susan L. "Staging Lope de Vega's *Peribáñez*: The Problem of an Ending." *Bulletin of Spanish Studies: Hispanic Studies and Researches on Spain, Portugal, and Latin America* 82, no. 2 (March 2005): 157–79.

Fox, Dian. *Refiguring the Hero: From Peasant to Noble in Lope De Vega and Calderón.* University Park: Pennsylvania State University Press, 1991.

———. "The Literary Use of History: *El médico de su honra* in Contexts." In *El arte nuevo de estudiar comedias: Literary Theory and Spanish Golden Age Drama*, edited by Barbara Simerka. Lewisburg, PA: Bucknell University Press and London: Associated University Presses, 1996.

Frye, Northrop. *Anatomy of Criticism: Four Essays.* Princeton, NJ: Princeton University Press, 1990.

Gaylord, Mary. "Amor y honor a traves del espejo." Edited by Luciano García Lorenzo. *Calderón: Actas del Congreso internacional sobre Calderón y el teatro español del Siglo de Oro.* Anejos de la Revista Segismundo: 6 (1983): 869–79.

———. "The Order in the Court: Cervantes' *Entremés del juez de los divorcios.*" *Bulletin of the Comediantes* 34, no. 1 (1982): 83–95.

González Echevarría, Roberto. *Celestina's Brood: Continuities of the Baroque in Spanish and Latin American Literatures.* Durham, NC: Duke University Press, 1993.

Greenblatt, Stephen. *Renaissance Self-Fashioning: From More to Shakespeare.* Chicago: University of Chicago Press, 1980.

Heath, Michael J. "Introductory Note." In *Collected Works of Erasmus. Institutio Christiani Matrimonii.* University of Toronto Press, 1974.

Howe, Elizabeth Teresa. *Education and Women in the Early Modern Hispanic World.* Women and gender in the early modern world. Aldershot, UK, and Burlington, VT: Ashgate Publishing, 2008.

Hufton, Olwen. "Women, Work, and Family." In *A History of Women: Renaissance and Enlightenment Paradoxes*, edited by Natalie Zemon Davis and Arlette Farge. Cambridge, MA: Harvard University Press, 1993.

Jorge García Reyes, Juan A. de. *El matrimonio de las minorías religiosas en el derecho español: Evolución histórica y regulación en la ley 7 de julio de 1981.* Madrid: Tecnos, 1986.

Kagan, Richard L., and Abigail Dyer. *Inquisitorial Inquiries: Brief Lives of Secret Jews and Other Heretics.* Baltimore: Johns Hopkins University Press, 2004.

Klapisch-Zuber, Christiane. *Women, Family, and Ritual in Renaissance Italy.* Chicago: University of Chicago Press, 1985.

León, Luis de. *A Bilingual Edition of Fray Luis de León's* La perfecta casada: *The Role of Married Women in Sixteenth-Century Spain.* Lewiston, NY: E. Mellen Press, 1999.

———. *Cantar de cantares*, edited by Jorge Guillén. Santiago de Chile: Editorial Cruz del Sur, 1947.

———. *Cantar de cantares de Salomón*, edited by José Manuel Blecua. Madrid: Gredos, 1994.

———. *Cantar de los cantares. Intepretaciones: Literal, espiritual, profética.* Madrid: Ediciones Escurialenses: Real Monasterio de El Escorial, 1992.

———. *De los nombres de Cristo*, edited by Cristóbal Cuevas García. Madrid: Ediciones Cátedra, 1977.

———. *Escritos desde la cárcel: Autógrafos del primer proceso inquisitorial.* Madrid: Ediciones Escurialenses, 1991.

Martínez-Góngora, Mar. *Discursos sobre la mujer en el humanismo renacentista español: los casos de Antonio de Guevara, Alfonso y Juan de Valdés y Luis de León.* York, SC: Spanish Literature Publications, 1999.

Mattingly, Garrett. *Catherine of Aragon.* Boston: Little, Brown, 1941.

McKendrick, Melveena. "Writings for the Stage." Pp. 131–59 in *The Cambridge Companion to Cervantes*, edited by Anthony J Cascardi. Cambridge, UK, and New York: Cambridge University Press, 2002.

Meehan, Andrew. "The Catholic Encyclopedia." www.newadvent.org/cathen/14441b.htm.

Noreña, Carlos. "Juan Luis Vives on the Relations between the Sexes." Pp. 449–61 in *Jewish Culture and the Hispanic World: Essays in Memory of Joseph H. Silverman*, edited by Samuel G Armistead, Mishael M. Caspi, and Murray Baumgarten. Newark, DE: Juan de la Cuesta, 2003.

Ortega y Gasset, José. *Vives-Goethe: Conferencias.* Madrid: Revista de Occidente, 1961.

Parker, Alexander Augustine. "Los amores y noviazgos clandestinos en el mundo dramático-social de Calderón." Pp. 79–87 in *Hacia Calderón. Segundo coloquio anglogermano Hamburgo.*, edited by Hans Flasche. Berlin and New York: W. de Gruyter, 1973.

Pinta Llorente, Miguel de la, and Palacio y de Palacio, José María de. *Procesos inquisitoriales contra la familia judía de Juan Luis Vives.* Madrid: Instituto Arias Montano, 1964.

Ratcliffe, Marjorie. "'Así que donde no hay varón, todo bien fallece': La viuda en la legislación medieval española." *Actas del X Congreso de la Asociacion de Hispanistas*, I–IV (1992): 311.

Reinhardt, Klaus. "Una exposición castellana del *Cantar de los cantares*, hasta ahora desconocida, atribuida a Fray Luis de León." Pp. 471–83 in *Fray Luis de León. Historia, humanismo y letras.*, edited by Víctor García de la Concha and Javier San José Lera. Salamanca: Ediciones Universidad, 1996.

Rivers, Elias L. "El mar en la poesía de Fray Luis de León." Pp. 315–18 in *Aspetti e problemi delle letterature iberiche: studi offerti a Franco Meregalli*, edited by Franco Meregalli. Roma: Bulzoni, 1981.

———. *Poesía lírica del Siglo De Oro.* Letras hispánicas. Madrid: Cátedra, 1991.

Rojas, Fernando de. *La Celestina*, edited by Dorothy Sherman Severin. Madrid: Cátedra, 1992.

Rueda, Lope de. *Pasos*, edited by José Luis Canet Vallés. Madrid: Editorial Castalia, 1992.

Ruiz de Conde, Justina. *El amor y el matrimonio secreto en los libros de caballerías*. Madrid: Aguilar, 1948.

Ruiz, Juan. *Libro de buen amor*, edited by Alberto Blecua. Barcelona: Planeta, 1983.

———. *The Book of Good Love*, translated by Elisha Kent Kane. Juan de la Cuesta Hispanic monographs. Newark, DE: Juan de la Cuesta, 2001.

Ruiz Ramón, Francisco. *Calderón nuestro contemporáneo*. Madrid: Editorial Castalia, 2000.

Saffar, Ruth. "Anxiety of Identity: Gutierre's Case in *El médico de su honra*." Pp. 105–24 in *Studies in Honor of Bruce W. Wardropper*, edited by Dian Fox, Harry Sieber, and Robert Ter Horst. Newark, DE: Juan de la Cuesta, 1989.

Salomon, Noël. *Lo villano en el teatro del Siglo de Oro*. Madrid: Ed. Castalia, 1985.

Schroeder, Henry Joseph. *Canons and Decrees of the Council of Trent*. Rockford, IL: Tan Books and Publishers, 1978.

Sepúlveda, Juan Ginés de. *Tratado sobre las justas causas de la guerra contra los indios*, edited by Manuel García-Pelayo. México: Fondo de Cultura Económica, 1987.

Sicroff, Albert A. *Los estatutos de limpieza de sangre: Controversias entre los siglos XV Y XVII*. Madrid: Taurus, 1985.

Soufas, Teresa Scott. "Calderón's Melancholy Wife-Murderers." *Hispanic Review* 52, no. 2 (1984): 181–203.

Spitzer, Leo. "Soy quien soy." *Nueva Revista Filologia Hispánica* 1 (1948): 113–27.

Telle, Émile Villemeur. *Érasme de Rotterdam et le septième sacrement: étude d'evangélisme matrimonial au XVI siècle et contribution a la biographie intellectuelle d'Érasme*. Geneva: Librairie E. Droz, 1954.

Thacker, Jonathan W. "Comedy's Social Compromise: Tirso's *Marta la piadosa* and the Refashioning of Role." *Bulletin of the Comediantes* 47, no. 2 (1995): 267–89.

Tierno Galván, Enrique. *Actas de las Cortes de Cádiz*. Madrid: Taurus, 1964.

Tobio, Constanza. "Marriage, Cohabitation and the Residential Independence of Young People in Spain." *Int J Law Policy Family* 15, no. 1 (April 1, 2001): 68–87.

Usunáriz, Jesús María. "El matrimonio como ejercicio de libertad en la España del siglo de oro." In *El matrimonio en Europa y el mundo hispánico. Siglos XVI y XVII*, edited by Ignacio Arellano. Madrid: Visor Libros, 2005.

Vasvari, Louise O. "Why Is Doña Endrina a Widow? Traditional Culture and Textuality in the *Libro de buen amor*." In *Upon My Husband's Death: Widows in the Literature and Histories of Medieval Europe*, edited by Louise Mirrer. Ann Arbor: University of Michigan Press, 1992.

Vega, Lope de. *Arte nuevo de hacer comedias*, edited by Enrique García Santo-Tomás. Madrid: Cátedra, 2006.

———. *La viuda valenciana*, edited by Teresa Ferrer. Madrid: Editorial Castalia, 2001.

———. *Peribáñez and the Comendador of Ocaña*, translated by James Lloyd. Aris & Phillips, 1990.

———. *Peribáñez y el Comendador de Ocaña*, edited by José M. Ruano de la Haza and J. E. Varey. London: Tamesis Texts, 1980.

———. *Peribáñez y el Comendador de Ocaña*, edited by Juan María Marín. Madrid: Cátedra, 2000.

Vitse, Marc. "Burla e ideología en los entremeses." Pp. 163–76 in *Los géneros menores en el teatro español del siglo de oro*, edited by Luciano García Lorenzo. Madrid: Ministerio de Cultura, 1988.

Vives, Juan Luis. *Instrucción de la mujer cristiana*, translated by Juan Justiniano. Madrid: Fundación Universitaria; Madrid: Universidad Pontificia de Salamanca, 1995.

———. *Obras completas*, translated by Llorenç Riber. Madrid: M. Aguilar, 1947.

———. *The Education of a Christian Woman: A Sixteenth-Century Manual*, translated by Charles Fantazzi. The Other Voice in Early Modern Europe. Chicago: University of Chicago Press, 2000.

———. *The Instruction of a Christen Woman*. Urbana: University of Illinois Press, 2002.

Wardropper, Bruce W. "Poetry and Drama in Calderón's *El médico de su honra*." *Romanic Review* 49 (1958): 3–11.

Wilson, E. M. "Image et structure dans 'Peribáñez.'" *Bulletin Hispanique* 51, no. 2 (1949): 125–59.

Zimic, Stanislav. "La ejemplaridad de los entremeses de Cervantes." *Bulletin of Hispanic Studies* 61, no. 3 (July 1984): 444–53.

tiempo, 122; *La dama boba*, 110; *Peribáñez y el Comendador de Ocaña*, xviii, 33–50; *La viuda valenciana*, xx–xxi, 98

La vida es sueño (Calderón), xi–xii, xxii, 72

Vega, Garcilaso de la, 111

violence: in *Médico de su honra*, 71–72, 74, 81; in *Peribáñez y el Comendador de Ocaña*, 35, 46, 49–50

virginity, xv

La viuda valenciana (Vega), xx–xxi, 97–115; contrast with conduct manuals, 105–6, 107; production of, 117n30; remarriage, 106; scholarship on, 106–7, 118n32; and sexuality, 107–8, 110, 114; and widowhood, 98

Vives, Juan Luis: and Catherine of Aragon, 1, 4; and Christianity, 5; *converso* status, 4, 5, 26n19; *Educación de la mujer cristiana*, xvii, 1–14; and marriage ideal, 14; *De officio mariti*, xix, 4; and sexuality, 3–4; on widowhood, 100–105, 115

wedding, 33–34

widowhood, 122; and attire, 103–4; and authority, 98, 103; behavior in, 101–5; as disadvantage, 99; and domesticity, 102; in *Education of the Christian Woman*, 100–105; and religious works, 105; and sexuality, 98, 100, 102–4, 105; in Spanish literature, 98–100; in *La viuda valenciana*, xx–xxi, 97–115

The Widow of Valencia (Vega). *See La viuda valenciana*

wife: expression of desire, 18, 59, 74–75; guides for, xvi, 2; ideal, 12, 21; how to choose, 8; metaphor of, 23–24; murder of, xx, 71–72, 74, 83, 88; obligations of, 20, 24, 36–39; role, 9, 21, 39; submission to husband, 14, 38

women: and cosmetics, 8–9; and dress, 7–8, 27n29, 41, 42–44, 103–4; and education, xvii, 2, 5–6, 12–13; and domesticity, 7, 20, 24; as readers, 16, 17, 20, 109–10; self-determination of, 12–13; subordination of, 8–9, 21

About the Author

Gabriela Carrión is assistant professor at Bard College where she teaches courses in Spanish language, literature, and culture. She received her PhD from Harvard University and her MA from the University of California at Berkeley. Her research examines sixteenth- and seventeenth-century Spanish literature and drama and focuses on questions of gender and sexuality in this period, with special attention to the works of Miguel de Cervantes, Lope de Vega, and Pedro Calderón de la Barca. She is currently working on the subject of humor and violence in Lope de Vega's *Los melindres de Belisa* as well as an edition and English translation of Antonio de Guevara's *Menosprecio de corte y alabanza de aldea* (*Disdain for the Court and Praise for the Countryside*).